CULTURES OF THE WORLD
Kyrgyzstan

Cavendish
Square
New York

Published in 2021 by Cavendish Square Publishing, LLC
243 5th Avenue, Suite 136, New York, NY 10016
Copyright © 2021 by Cavendish Square Publishing, LLC

Third Edition

Website: cavendishsq.com

This publication represents the opinions and views of the author based on his or her personal experience, knowledge, and research. The information in this book serves as a general guide only. The author and publisher have used their best efforts in preparing this book and disclaim liability rising directly or indirectly from the use and application of this book.

All websites were available and accurate when this book was sent to press.

Library of Congress Cataloging-in-Publication Data

Names: King, David C., author. | Nevins, Debbie, author.
Title: Kyrgyzstan / David C. King and Debbie Nevins.
Description: Third edition. | New York : Cavendish Square Publishing,
 [2021] | Series: Cultures of the world | Includes bibliographical
 references and index.
Identifiers: LCCN 2020022290 | ISBN 9781502658722 (library binding) | ISBN
 9781502658739 (ebook)
Subjects: LCSH: Kyrgyzstan—Juvenile literature.
Classification: LCC DK913 .K55 2021 | DDC 958.43--dc23
LC record available at https://lccn.loc.gov/2020022290

Writers, third edition: David C. King and Debbie Nevins
Editor, third edition: Debbie Nevins
Designer, third edition: Jessica Nevins
Picture Researcher, third edition: Jessica Nevins

PICTURE CREDITS

The photographs in this book are used with the permission of: Cover ugurhan/E+/Getty Images; p. 1 toiletroom/Shutterstock.com; pp. 3, 80 Frank De Luyck/Gallo Images/Getty Images Plus; p. 5 Omri Eliyahu/Shutterstock.com; p. 7, 31, 84, 106, 112, 118 Vyacheslav Oseledko/AFP via Getty Images; p. 8 DavorLovincic/E+/Getty Images; p. 10 Jaap Hooijkaas/Moment/Getty Images; p. 12 Belkina Natalia/iStock/Getty Images Plus; p. 14 Jeremy Woodhouse/DigitalVision/Getty Images; p. 15 Aureliy/iStock/Getty Images Plus; p. 16 Aibek Melisov/EyeEm/Getty Images; p. 17 Hramovnick/iStock/Getty Images Plus; p. 18 Kylie Nicholson/Shutterstock.com; p. 20 Anthony Plummer/Lonely Planet Images/Getty Images Plus; p. 22 Pool Benainous/Tinacci/Gamma-Rapho via Getty Images; p. 25 PeterHermesFurian/iStock/Getty Images Plus; p. 27 Touring Club Italiano/Marka/Universal Images Group via Getty Images; p. 28 Bonn-Sequenz/ullstein bild via Getty Images; p. 34 Martin Moos/Lonely Planet Images/Getty Images Plus; p. 37 Travel Ink/Gallo Images/Getty Images Plus; p. 40 Oseledko/AFP via Getty Images; p. 42 Andrew Caballero-Reynolds/Getty Images; p. 44 Jeremy Woodhouse/Lonely Planet Images/Getty Images Plus; p. 45 Viktor Drachev\TASS via Getty Images; p. 46 Hermes Images/AGF/Universal Images Group via Getty Images; p. 47 Taylor Weidman/Bloomberg via Getty Images; p. 48 Vladimir_Pirogov312/iStock Editorial/Getty Images Plus; p. 49 Radist/iStock/Getty Images Plus; p. 50 DavorLovincic/E+/Getty Images; p. 52 outcast85/iStock/Getty Images Plus; p. 54 Alan Sau/Shutterstock.com; p. 56 Kirill Skorobogatko/Shutterstock.com; pp. 58, 101 Johnny Haglund/Lonely Planet Images/Getty Images Plus; p. 60 Rui T. Guedes/Shutterstock.com; p. 62 Frans Sellies/Contributor/Moment Editorial/Getty Images; p. 64 Matyas Rehak/Shutterstock.com; p. 68 Frank De Luyck/Gallo Images/Getty Images Plus; p. 70 Oliver Foerstner/Shutterstock.com; pp. 72, 74, 126 Radiokafka/Shutterstock.com; p. 73 Mathias Rhode/iStock/Getty Images Plus; pp. 75, 128 Michal Knitl/Shutterstock.com; p. 77 Nevada Wier/The Image Bank/Getty Images Plus; pp. 78, 114, 116 Maximum Exposure PR/Shutterstock.com; p. 82 Neal J. Wilson/Moment/Getty Images; p. 88 Alex Skachkov/Shutterstock.com; p. 89 Omurali Toichiev/Shutterstock.com; pp. 90, 95 Eric Valenne geostory/Shutterstock.com; p. 92 Amos Chapple/Lonely Planet Images/Getty Images Plus; p. 98 Suresh Krishna/Contributor/Moment/Getty Images; pp. 102, 104, 127 MehmetO/Shutterstock.com; p. 103 Brill/ullstein bild via Getty Images; p. 108 Tuul & Bruno Morandi/The Image Bank Unreleased/Getty Images; p. 109 Fredy Thuerig/Shutterstock.com; p. 110 tunart/E+./Getty Images; p. 111 Katiekk/Shutterstock.com; p. 120 karenfoleyphotography/Shutterstock.com; p. 122 Darya Ufimtseva/iStock/Getty Images Plus; p. 124 Vladimir Pirogov/Shutterstock.com; p. 130 Oleg Golovnev/Shutterstock.com; p. 131 Fanfo/Shutterstock.com.

Some of the images in this book illustrate individuals who are models. The depictions do not imply actual situations or events.

CPSIA compliance information: Batch #CW21CSQ: For further information contact Cavendish Square Publishing LLC, New York, New York, at 1-877-980-4450.

Printed in the United States of America

Find us on

CONTENTS

KYRGYZSTAN TODAY

TUCKED BETWEEN ITS TWO MASSIVE NEIGHBORS, CHINA AND Kazakhstan, the small nation of Kyrgyzstan (KUR-gih-stahn) tends to fly below the radar of many Westerners. It's one of the five "'Stans" that make up Central Asia, the vast expanse of terrain that lies between China and Europe. *Stan* is a Persian word that means "land of," and Kazakhstan, Kyrgyzstan, Tajikistan, Turkmenistan, and Uzbekistan are named for the ethnic peoples who live in them. (There are other "'Stans," some more familiar to Westerners—Afghanistan, Pakistan, and others—but strictly speaking, they are outside of Central Asia.)

The Kyrgyz Republic, as it's officially named, is a land of astonishing beauty, with snowcapped mountains, windswept deserts, and grass-covered steppes. Most of the nation's 6 million people now live in settled communities, but for thousands of years, their ancestors were nomads, moving their herds of horses, sheep, and camels in a constant search for new grazing pastures.

Long ago, this region served as a launching pad for the armies of nomadic warriors—mainly the Huns and later, the "Golden Horde" of Genghis Khan—in their campaigns of conquest. Kyrgyzstan was also an outpost along the Silk Road, a historic caravan route that made possible the transfer of goods, ideas, and technologies between East and West.

In those days, national borders didn't exist, since most of the people were nomadic. They did not own land in any legal sense. They simply roamed where their ancestors had roamed, knowing the geography of the place intimately. Indeed, there was no formal land known as Kyrgyzstan. This country is a relatively new invention, dating back only about a century.

In the late 19th century, the czarist Russian Empire expanded southward, taking what territories it wanted. In the early 20th century, that empire was violently replaced by another, the Communist Soviet Union. Central Asia was forged into Soviet states. The nomads were forced to settle down and radically change their lifestyles. Soviet dictator Joseph Stalin drew new, somewhat arbitrary boundaries for administrative purposes that corresponded neither to natural geographic features nor to the ethnic identities of the people living within them.

This new place called Kyrgyzstan existed for 70 years as a Soviet republic. It became in many ways an extension of Russia. The Kyrgyz people learned to speak Russian, adopted Russian traditions, and learned to rely on the Communist central government in Moscow. All that fell apart as the Soviet Union finally collapsed, and Kyrgyzstan emerged from the ashes as an independent entity in 1991.

Since that time, Kyrgyzstan has tried to reinvent itself as a modern democratic country. It hasn't been an easy task. Kyrgyzstanis have tried to salvage their own identity by reaching back to their heritage, but they can't turn back the clock. They are proud of their nomadic traditions but can't all revert to being nomads once again. However, they are still largely a rural people. Many embrace a semi-nomadic life, staying put for most of the year but moving with their flocks to high summer pastures in the mountains.

The idea of nationhood still feels foreign to some of the country's citizens. There is an ethnic and cultural division between the north and the south, reinforced geographically by high mountain ranges. In the north live most of the ethnic Kyrgyz, while the south is populated more by ethnic Uzbeks. Many people feel more allegiance to their locality than to the nation as a whole. It doesn't help that the north tends to do better economically and holds more political power than the south. This makes frictions heat up.

In the 21st century, the Kyrgyzstanis have already staged two revolutions, in 2005 and 2010. Public demonstrations succeeded in throwing out the existing government; each time, the president was accused of corruption. This problem still muddies the political climate today, and Kyrgyzstan's international reputation as an emerging democracy seems increasingly uncertain.

In March 2020, the global COVID-19 pandemic reached Kyrgyzstan. The cities of Bishkek, Osh, and Jalal-Abad went into emergency lockdown to prevent the spread of the virus. By June 2020, there were 3,356 confirmed cases of COVID-19 with 40 deaths in the country. Kyrgyzstan was the first country to receive emergency funding from the International Monetary Fund (IMF) to help it cope with the outbreak. The IMF said at the time its board had approved an emergency $121 million disbursement to Kyrgyzstan. How the situation will play out, and what its aftereffects will be, remain to be seen.

A medic checks people's temperatures at a checkpoint outside Bishkek, the capital of Kyrgyzstan, as the city tries to prevent the spread of COVID-19 on April 1, 2020.

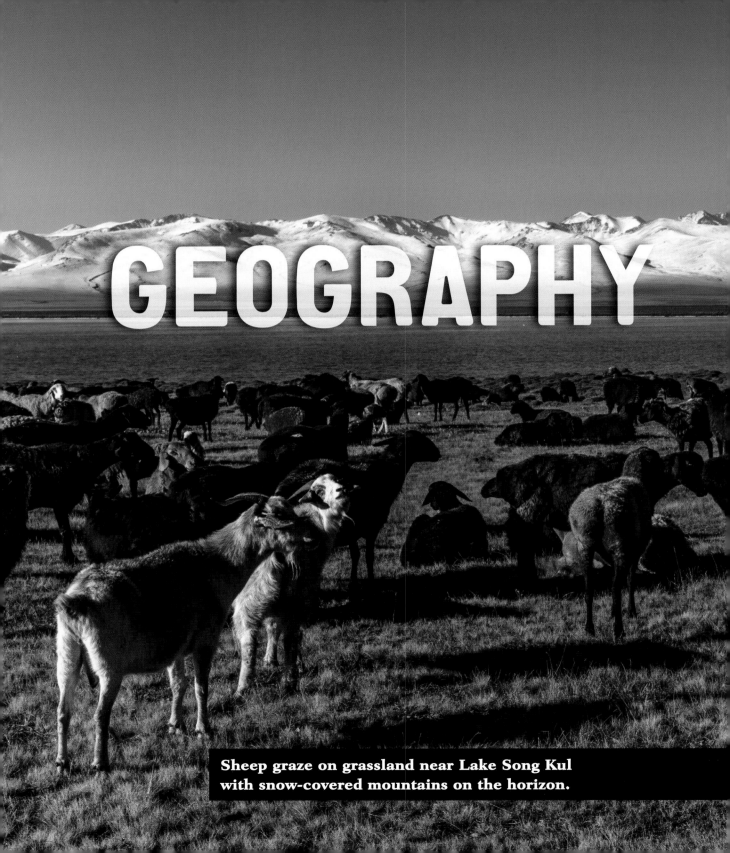

GEOGRAPHY

Sheep graze on grassland near Lake Song Kul with snow-covered mountains on the horizon.

1

KYRGYZSTAN IS ONE OF THE smallest Central Asian countries. "Small" in this sense is a relative description. Surrounded by enormous nations, Kyrgyzstan is only about the size of South Dakota, the 17th-largest U.S. state, which is far from small.

On a map or a globe, though, Kyrgyzstan seems almost lost in the colossal mountain ranges of Central Asia. Tucked within the folds of these various mountains, this former Soviet republic covers an area of 77,202 square miles (199,951 sq kilometers). Three other former Soviet republics border Kyrgyzstan—Kazakhstan to the north; Uzbekistan to the west; and Tajikistan to the south. China is Kyrgyzstan's neighbor to the east.

Two mountain ranges, the Tian Shan, or Tien Shan, ("Mountains of Heaven") and the Pamir, dominate the country. They cover about 65 percent of the land area and give Kyrgyzstan an average altitude of 9,803 feet (2,988 meters)—about 1.8 miles (2.9 km) above sea level. Lake Issyk-Kul, one of the world's largest mountain lakes, nestles in a basin 1 mile (1.6 km) above sea level. The country is landlocked; it has no coastline and does not come into direct contact with the sea.

MOUNTAINS AND STEPPES

The mountains of Kyrgyzstan and its bordering nations are known to geologists as the Pamir Knot—the hub from which different ranges radiate like the spokes of a wheel. These mountains were created millions of

Kyrgyzstan is not only landlocked but also farther from the sea than any other individual country. Even its rivers do not reach the sea but rather flow into lakes or swamps, where the waters evaporate or seep into the soil.

years ago when the shifting of the planet's tectonic plates caused the Indian subcontinent to collide with the Asian landmass.

The force of this collision pushed the land up into some of the world's mightiest mountain ranges, including the Himalaya, Hindu Kush, and Tian Shan mountains. The process that created the towering peaks began around 100 million years ago and has not stopped since. The Tian Shan mountains continue to grow, gaining altitude at the rate of a few inches per year.

The Tian Shan, with their network of intervening valleys and basins, stretch about 1,500 miles (2,415 km) in an east-west direction, spanning a width of 220 to 300 miles (354 to 483 km). The highest peaks are in the middle of the range. Pobeda Peak (also known as Jengish Chokusu) is the tallest, reaching a height of 24,400 feet (7,437 m).

Different mountain elevations produce many kinds of soil and vegetation. Diverse species of animals also make their homes in the varied habitats found at different altitudes. The most common landscape is the steppe. Similar to the prairie grasslands of North America, the steppe is a virtually unbroken

Views like this one in the Karakol Valley attract hikers from around the world.

prairie that stretches from Hungary and Poland in Eastern Europe across Central Asia to China.

For more than 2,000 years, the steppe was home to nomadic tribes. Some, on horseback, formed powerful armies, using the speed and mobility of their cavalries to conquer vast areas. The great Mongol emperor Genghis Khan amassed one of history's most powerful empires in this way.

VALLEYS AND LOWLANDS

Most of the Kyrgyzstani people live in the lowland areas, which make up only one-seventh of the total area of this nation.

THE CHUY VALLEY   This valley in the north Tian Shan mountains of Kyrgyzstan is a large, flat region watered by the Chu (also known as Chuy or Chui) River and its tributaries. The valley is one of the country's most fertile agricultural regions and among its most densely populated areas. The nation's capital, Bishkek, is located in this valley region.

THE FERGANA VALLEY   This sprawling area of grassland in the southwest stretches into Uzbekistan and Tajikistan. About one out of every five Kyrgyz live in this region. Kyrgyzstan's second-largest city, Osh, with 281,900 inhabitants, is located here and is popularly known as the "capital of the South."

The valley forms a green oasis walled in by a different mountain range on each side. For nearly 2,000 years, a main artery of the Silk Road passed through the area. Before that, the kingdom of Fergana was famed for its "heavenly" horses—swift, elegant creatures believed to be the ancestors of today's Arabian horses.

During the years of Soviet rule, the Communist leaders in Moscow were determined to remake Central Asia. This goal was part of a massive plan to have each part of the Soviet Union contribute specific products or resources to the welfare of the entire empire. The scheme was devised in order to reduce overproduction and waste.

The Moscow planners wanted the Fergana Valley to become a major area for cotton production. To do this, grazing land was plowed under, and rivers

Wild horses graze in a sunny meadow in the mountains of Kyrgyzstan.

were dammed to provide suitable irrigation. Chemical fertilizers and pesticides were used liberally to increase production.

Workers in the valley were soon harvesting thousands of tons of cotton every year, but the experiment was ultimately harmful to both the economy and the environment. When the Soviet Union began to collapse, the market for Kyrgyz cotton collapsed with it, leading to widespread unemployment and poverty. The Kyrgyz government and people are still searching for solutions.

THE SUUSAMYR VALLEY   This is one of the major features marking central Kyrgyzstan. The area is made up of a high steppe plateau bordered to the north and south by vast high-elevation snowfields, with deep rivers slicing through its center. Harsh winters and the rugged terrain make this a poor farming region, best used for grazing sheep and horses. During the Soviet era, when farms operated as large collectives, as many as 4 million sheep grazed the valley. In today's harder economic climate, that number has fallen to fewer than 1 million. Instead, many families are trying to grow hardy vegetables such as potatoes and cabbages. In addition, the cool air and beautiful scenery of the high pastures in summer are drawing more and more tourists. Families offer "homestays," providing lodging for visitors who are attracted to the idea of sleeping in a yurt (a domed tent) instead of in a resort lodge.

RIVERS AND LAKES

The meltwater from high mountain glaciers feeds most of the country's rivers and many of its more than 1,900 lakes. The Engilchek Glacier, one of the world's largest, is located in an area of gigantic glaciers called Muztag ("Ice Mountain") by the Kyrgyz. Every summer enough ice melts to form Lake Merzbacher, a large lake surrounded by an ice dam. It's often called the "Disappearing Lake" because it drains away in August, after its ice banks fracture and crumble, causing a glacial lake outburst flood that showers icebergs into the Engilchek River below.

Although Krygyzstan has a wealth of rivers and streams—upwards of 40,000—they are mostly not navigable. They are, however, a great source of hydroelectricity, and there are numerous dams and reservoirs built on a number of rivers for this purpose. One of them is the Naryn River, the country's longest river, at 501 miles (807 km). It rises in the Tian Shan mountains in the eastern part of the country and flows west through the Fergana Valley into Uzbekistan.

LAKE ISSYK-KUL ("WARM LAKE")   This is the country's largest body of water. It's the seventh-deepest lake in the world, and the tenth-largest by volume, though not by area. Along with the central Tian Shan mountains, the lake covers most of eastern Kyrgyzstan. It lies at the bottom of a large depression, or basin, about 150 miles (242 km) long and 45 miles (72 km) wide. This is a warm, dry area. July temperatures along the lakeshore average 62 degrees Fahrenheit (17 degrees Celsius). In January, the average temperature is 28°F (-2°C).

Bishkek, the capital, is by far the largest city in the republic, with a population of about one million people. Formerly named Pishpek, it was renamed Frunze in 1926, during the Soviet era, after the Bolshevik military leader Mikhail Frunze, who was born there. In 1991, the newly independent Kyrgyz parliament changed the capital's name to Bishkek.

Today it's the nation's hub of business and industry, as well as the seat of government, and it has the greatest mixture of ethnic and national groups in the country. Throughout the 20th century, most of the people in the city were ethnic Europeans—Russians, Germans, and

The mountains of the Kyrgyz Range rise beyond Bishkek, with the city's Victory Square in the foreground.

Ukrainians. Today, however, it is predominantly ethnic Kyrgyz, with Europeans making up less than 20 percent. Nevertheless, the Russian language is the dominant tongue.

Although it was once an ancient settlement on the Silk Road, the city itself is quite new. The Russian government built it in the late 1800s and encouraged Russian peasants to settle in the region, where they could farm the fertile valley. The appearance of the city itself is more Russian than Asian. The broad streets were laid out in a grid pattern by Russian planners, making it easy to get around. Residential areas feature Russian- and Ukrainian-style houses, with curved eaves and gardens of apricot, apple, and shade trees. Stately oak trees grace the parks and line the major streets.

Architecturally, few of the buildings predate World War II (1939–1945). During the 1970s and 1980s, the Soviets' Communist leadership oversaw construction of the impressive city center, Ala-Too Square, with its monumental buildings. The city's bazaars, or marketplaces, are always busy. The huge, colorful Osh Bazaar is a major shopping center, and the Dordoy Bazaar is like a gigantic flea market, filled with people and alive with activity. It is made up of thousands of shipping containers trucked into the city and double stacked.

The lake itself is 113 miles (182 km) long and 38 miles (61 km) wide. Famous for the fact that it never freezes (due to its salinity), it is just as well known for its sky-blue color and high mineral content. In fact, the water is so full of minerals that it is unsafe for human consumption, although people sometimes use its water for their cattle.

Around 118 rivers and streams flow into the lake, with the largest being the Tyup and the Jyrgalan Rivers. The lake is also fed by springs, including many hot springs, and snow melt. It has no outlet.

LAKE SONG KUL   This remote mountain lake in the Naryn Province is the country's second-largest lake. Because it is so difficult to access, the beautiful lake has no tourist facilities. However, the area has become popular with herders, who can take advantage of the lush pastures and a lake filled with fish.

Lake Issyk-Kul in eastern Kyrgyzstan was a popular vacation destination in Soviet times.

The snowcapped Tian Shan mountains create a frozen landscape in the Naryn Region, or Province, of Kyrgyzstan.

CLIMATE

Kyrgyzstan's location, in the heart of the great Eurasian landmass, gives it a continental climate, characterized by short, hot summers and long, cold winters. Because of the mountainous terrain, there are wide fluctuations in temperature and weather conditions, even within the same region. A valley area, for example, might average 60°F (15°C) in July, while higher up a mountain slope the average could be 45°F (7°C). Still higher, a mountain pass might dip below freezing at night, even in July. Although the mountain peaks are often shrouded in clouds, Kyrgyzstan is a surprisingly sunny country. There is an average of 247 sunny days each year.

The nation's weather can range from fiercely cold to extremely hot. The first snows of winter close the mountain passes by November, and the bitter cold continues through February. Freezing temperatures at night can continue into May or even longer at higher elevations.

Spring birds appear in March, April, or May, again depending on the altitude. From late June through mid-August, afternoon temperatures reach 90°F (32°C) or higher, although mountain valleys tend to be cooler. Like the temperature, precipitation varies considerably in different parts of the mountain ranges. In general, most of the rainfall comes in spring and early summer.

FLORA AND FAUNA

Kyrgyzstan is home to a wealth of plant and animal life. The many mountain ranges provide a variety of habitats. Forests of walnut and pistachio trees, as well as varieties of almond, apple, pear, cherry, and pomegranate trees, blanket the lower slopes in the south. The northern mountains are covered with forests of juniper and Tian Shan pine trees.

Mountain wildflowers blanket a sunny meadow in the Pamir region of southern Kyrgyzstan.

Since 1975, the United Nations Educational, Scientific and Cultural Organization (UNESCO) has maintained a list of international landmarks or regions considered to be of "outstanding value" to the people of the world. Such sites embody the common natural and cultural heritage of humanity, and therefore deserve particular protection. The organization works with the host country to establish plans for managing and conserving their sites. UNESCO also reports on sites that are in imminent or potential danger of destruction and can offer emergency funds to try to save the property.

The organization is continually assessing new sites for inclusion on the World Heritage List. In order to be selected, a site must be of "outstanding universal value" and meet at least one of ten criteria. These required elements include cultural value—that is, artistic, religious, or historical significance—and natural value, including exceptional beauty, unusual natural phenomena, and scientific importance.

As of 2020, there were 1,121 sites listed: 869 cultural, 213 natural, and 39 mixed (cultural and natural) properties in 167 nations. Of those, 53 are listed as "in danger."

Kyrgyzstan has two cultural sites and one natural site listed. Only one, the cultural Sulaiman-Too Sacred Mountain, is exclusive to Kyrgyzstan. The two others are transnational

Sulaiman-Too ("Solomon's Throne") Sacred Mountain, a sacred location near the city of Osh in the Fergana Valley, is Kyrgyzstan's sole exclusive World Heritage Site.

properties shared with other countries. The cultural listing called "Silk Roads: the Routes Network of Chang'an-Tianshan Corridor" includes sections of Kyrgyzstan, China, and Kazakhstan. The natural listing for the "Western Tien-Shan" mountain region is made up of multiple locations. Four of its thirteen locations are in Kyrgyzstan, while the others are in Kazakhstan and Uzbekistan.

Kyrgyzstan has submitted two more selections for World Heritage consideration, and they are on the Tentative List.

The amazing diversity in plant life includes an estimated 400 species found only in Kyrgyzstan. In spring and summer, there is a colorful procession of wildflowers, including many kinds of tulips and other bulb plants, such as anemones, crocuses, and colchicums.

Animal life is also widely varied. The open steppe lands support antelope, roe deer, ground squirrels, and European red squirrels. Mountain regions are home to ibex, various kinds of marmots, and rare Marco Polo sheep with their unusual curved horns. Most big cats, including tigers and cheetahs, are no longer found in Kyrgyzstan, but a rare snow leopard is sometimes seen. In fact, the Sarychat Ertash State Nature Reserve, high up in the Tian Shan mountains, is one of Kyrgyzstan's prime snow leopard habitats. The forested mountain slopes also provide the ideal habitat for wild boars, brown bears, lynxes, wolves, and foxes.

Bird life is just as abundant, with more than 360 species making their homes in Kyrgyzstan, including European birds as well as species common to China and other parts of Asia. There is a wide variety of raptors, including imperial eagles; the rare black vulture; and the lammergeier, an eagle-like vulture with a wingspan of nearly 10 feet (3 m). The wetlands provide habitats for many kinds of wild fowl as well.

INTERNET LINKS

http://factsanddetails.com/central-asia/Kyrgyzstan/sub8_5e/entry-4798.html
A basic overview of the land, geography, and weather of Kyrgyzstan is offered on this site.

https://www.remotelands.com/country/Kyrgyzstan
This travel site provides an overview of Kyrgyzstan's regions.

https://whc.unesco.org/en/statesparties/kg
This is the UNESCO World Heritage page for Kyrgyzstan.

HISTORY

The Burana Tower, the ruins of an 11th-century minaret, is all that remains of the ancient city of Balasagun in the Chuy Valley, about 50 miles (80 km) east of Bishkek.

2

THE HISTORY OF KYRGYZSTAN IS the history of Central Asia. Historians can't really separate the two. The boundaries that delineate Kyrgyzstan on maps today were largely created last century by the Soviet Union to serve the political needs of its dictator, Joseph Stalin. The history of this newly minted nation is the story of a region that has seen its share of turmoil and change.

Archaeological evidence indicates that people first arrived in Central Asia about 30,000 years ago. Some of the most exciting finds in today's Kyrgyzstan include the discovery of thousands of petroglyphs (prehistoric rock carvings) created by Bronze Age peoples, beginning about 5,000 years ago. In 1902, more than 10,000 petroglyphs were found around a place called Saimaluu Tash, sometimes spelled Saymaly-Tash, ("Embroidered Stones") on the slopes of Mount Suleiman. The drawings and carvings, often made with considerable skill, depict animals as well as scenes of hunting, farming, and ritual dancing.

NOMADIC EMPIRES

The first identifiable societies in Central Asia were warlike clans known as the Scythians (or Sakas). They first arrived in the region in the ninth and eighth centuries BCE. The Scythians lived in semi-settled communities,

In 1876, the Russian Empire took over much of what is now Kyrgyzstan. In 1916, the Kyrgyz people staged a revolt against Russia, in which one-sixth of the Kyrgyz population was killed. A civil war in Russia led to the establishment of the Communist Soviet Union. Kyrgyzstan became a Soviet republic in 1936. Even though Kyrgyzstan became independent in 1991, the Russian language and culture still have a strong presence in Kyrgyzstani life.

This 1865 map on Japanese fabric shows land and sea routes of the Silk Road.

combining farming and herding. However, they were best known as warriors, a highly mobile army whose swift horses helped them overwhelm established towns and farm villages. The Scythians built the first of a series of empires ruled by nomadic warriors that was to last more than a thousand years.

Beginning in the second century BCE, the Scythians maintained peace in the region that was crisscrossed by the caravan routes collectively known as the Silk Road. Around the first century, the Scythians were gradually forced eastward by Persian armies and slowly faded from history.

Around the fourth century, another group of nomadic clans—the Huns—swept across the steppes and mountains of Central Asia, reaching as far west as the Volga River. Under their determined leader, Attila, the Huns pushed onward into Rome, having a hand in the eventual downfall of the Roman Empire.

THE SILK ROAD: CROSSROADS OF EAST AND WEST

In 138 BCE, when the Chinese general Chang Chien traveled west to the Fergana Valley in search of the powerful horses he had heard so much about, he did not realize he was establishing one of history's legendary trade routes.

The Silk Road, as it came to be called, was more than one route; it was a network, or corridor, of correlating trails that crossed the vast expanse of Central Asia. It linked East to West, connecting and opening up once-distant realms, hastening the exchange of their various goods, ideas, technologies, and religious beliefs.

With two great civilizations—China and Europe—at the opposite ends of the Silk Road, Kyrgyzstan occupied a key position in the middle of the great commercial route. Along inhospitable mountain trails and across harsh plateaus, caravans would wind their way to the West, bringing silks, tea, spices, perfumes, medicines, paper, jade, porcelain, and dyes. The traders going east brought horses, camels, and other animals; wine and grapes; linen and wool; glassware; weapons and armor; slaves; and gold and other precious metals.

The caravans also carried more than mere goods—the ideas, arts, religions, and technologies that were spread enriched both cultures. The East gained exposure to Christianity, Judaism, and the art and music of Europe. China received Nestorian Christianity (a branch of the faith that broke off from Byzantine Christianity in the 430s) and Buddhism (from India) via the Silk Road. Meanwhile, merchants spread Islam throughout the mountainous regions. The West learned about printing, paper money, and gunpowder.

Although the Silk Road waxed and waned as a route for transporting goods and ideas, it was revived in the 13th and 14th centuries with the travels of Marco Polo (1254–1324). The Venetian merchant traveled along the Silk Road with camels laden with goods. Sea routes eventually proved more efficient, but the land routes still exist today in parts.

The National Historical Museum in Bishkek contains such relics as a third-century scrap of silk, Chinese coins, Indian cowrie-shell bracelets, iron swords, bronze lamps and amulets, and stone Nestorian crosses—all of which attest to the international nature of the route.

In 560 CE, the Huns were beaten by the Turks at Talas, in northwestern Kyrgyzstan, and, like the Scythians, they soon disappeared as a unified, organized society. Various clans of nomadic Turks maintained control over most of Central Asia in the sixth and seventh centuries. They established peaceful relations with the Sogdians—people of Persian (Iranian) ancestry who were farmers and Silk Road traders. The Turks were the first group in Central Asia to leave written records and the first to mention tribes called the Kyrgyz, who were then living in Siberia (central and eastern Russia).

From about 650 to 750, the Turks and their Sogdian allies managed to hold back the powerful armies of the Arab Muslims who came from the West. Ultimately, they joined forces with the Arabs to beat a large Chinese army advancing from the East. In 751, at the Talas River in today's Kyrgyzstan, the Turks, Sogdians, and Arabs defeated the Chinese. The event proved significant because it ended the growing Chinese influence in the region. Islamic law and culture would dominate the area from then on.

Over the next three to four centuries, the Kyrgyz people gradually moved south into present-day Kyrgyzstan, pressed by the relentless advance of another society of nomadic clans—the Mongols. In their new home in Central Asia, the Kyrgyz became known as shrewd traders and as tough warriors, combining skill in horsemanship with great stamina.

THE MONGOL EMPIRE

In the early 13th century, the world witnessed the rise of one of history's most feared empires. The Mongol epoch began when a tribal leader named Temujin, who became better known as Genghis Khan, managed to unite the Mongol clans into the most efficient army of mounted warriors the world had ever seen. Genghis Khan used brilliant battlefield tactics and may have been the first to use military maneuvers and war games to train his warriors and refine his strategy.

Genghis Khan began his conquest of Central Asia in 1219 and soon gained control of every oasis city along the Silk Road. He was merciless in his treatment of any peoples who offered resistance. Much of Central Asia was inhabited by fiercely independent groups, mostly nomads who tried to resist the khan's domination. Hundreds of thousands died at the hands of his "Golden Horde."

The Kyrgyz made up one of the groups that tried to fight the Mongols, but they were soon overwhelmed and nearly wiped out. Most then joined forces with Genghis Khan's armies, working as mercenaries, fighting for pay.

Genghis Khan and his armies were known for their ruthless nature and their vicious, violent assaults. He destroyed cities, burning buildings and butchering thousands of innocent people in the process. However, he gradually came to see the importance of cities and, late in his life, allowed trade to flourish again.

Genghis Khan's empire, based in China, eventually spread across Asia reaching the Caspian Sea. After his death in 1227, his sons continued to expand the empire, but the Mongol armies were unable to establish a foothold in Europe. In the late 1200s, the famous Italian traveler Marco Polo crossed Asia on the Silk Road and spent several years in the Chinese court of Kublai Khan, Genghis Khan's grandson. Polo's account of the fabulous wealth of China and Japan made the people of Europe curious about these mysterious and previously unheard-of places. The hope of finding a sea route to these lands was one of the main forces driving Europe's Age of Exploration.

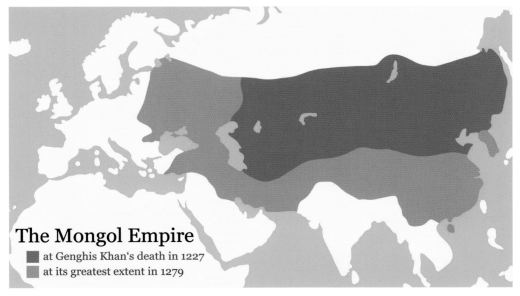

The Mongol Empire
■ at Genghis Khan's death in 1227
■ at its greatest extent in 1279

This map shows the expanse of the Mongol Empire at the time of Genghis Khan's death in 1227, at which time it included the Kyrgyzstan region, and at its greatest extent in 1279.

In the late 1300s, another conqueror tried to emulate Genghis Khan's notorious career of war and plunder. Born in the region of today's Uzbekistan, this tyrant was named Timur and became known to history as Timur the Lame, or Tamerlane. In a nine-year period, he laid waste to most of present-day Iran, Iraq, Syria, Turkey, and northern India. Tamerlane and his grandson built a fabulous capital at Samarqand in Uzbekistan, making it a major city along the Silk Road as well as a center of learning.

THE ARRIVAL OF THE RUSSIANS

Following the breakup of Tamerlane's empire, Central Asia entered a period of disorder and economic decline that stretched into the 16th and 17th centuries. The last of the nomadic rulers controlled three separate kingdoms, or khanates. Europeans had opened sea routes to Asia, causing a sharp decline in the traffic on the Silk Road.

In the 18th and early 19th centuries, the people who would eventually be known as the Kyrgyz found themselves cornered in their mountain strongholds, overtaken and ruled by the Kokand khanate (1709–1876), which was Uzbek. It was during this time that Islam began to be introduced to the Kyrgyz, who gradually adopted it.

When Russian armies began moving into Central Asia, the Kyrgyz turned to them for help. In the mid-1860s, Russian and Kyrgyz troops defeated the Kokand forces. Tashkent (today the capital of Uzbekistan) fell under Russian control, then Samarqand (an ancient Uzbek city not far from the Kyrgyzstan border) and Kyrgyzstan.

The government of czarist Russia thought of Kyrgyzstan as a colony that could provide land and opportunity for Russians, as well as for several thousand Ukrainians and Germans. The Kyrgyz watched the Russians make many improvements, but these benefited the newcomers, not the region's native residents. Russians were also allowed to take "unoccupied" lands, but most of those lands had been used seasonally by Kyrgyz herders for grazing.

The Kyrgyz tolerated the increasingly intrusive and heavy-handed Russian rule until 1916, when they launched a revolt that was ruthlessly put down by the Russians. Out of about 750,000 Kyrgyz, 120,000 were killed and another

120,000 fled to China. Following the Communist Revolution of 1917 to 1918, which transformed Russia into the Soviet Union, the lands of the defeated Kyrgyz were made part of the Turkestan Autonomous Soviet Socialist Republic (ASSR). Not until 1936 did Kyrgyzstan become a full Soviet socialist republic (SSR) called Kirghiziya.

UNDER SOVIET RULE

Nomadic Kyrgyz suffered heavily under the rule of the Soviets, especially when the dictator Joseph Stalin launched his land reforms. Starting in the 1920s, groups of nomads were forced to live in settled communities. Then, between 1928 and 1932, thousands were compelled to live on large farms called collectives. To the Kyrgyz, the idea of giving up their grazing lands and their herds struck at the very heart of their nomadic way of life. Many responded by slaughtering millions of horses, camels, and sheep; thousands fled to China. Opposition to this new lifestyle was cruelly suppressed, and by 1932, the collective farms had been firmly established.

This photograph shows a typical Kyrgyz dwelling from the 1920s, when the nomads were forced to settle into communities.

Askar Akayev, President of the Kyrgyz Republic from 1990 to 2005, is shown here in 1992.

In the late 1930s, Stalin launched another campaign—to purge the Soviet Union of all those suspected of being nationalists (retaining loyalty to their home region) or capitalists. Several hundred Kyrgyz, including members of the intelligentsia (the social and intellectual elite) and some *akyns* (traditional songwriter-performers), were rounded up and sent to prison camps in Siberia. Some Kyrgyz citizens were shot by the secret police.

During World War II, thousands of Kyrgyz died fighting in the Soviet armies against the German invaders. Some scholars believe that half of the troops from Central Asia defected to the German side. When Germans advanced deep into Soviet territory, entire factories were moved—along with their complete staffs of workers—to the safety of Kyrgyzstan. This boosted the country's industrial base but also placed the country largely under Russian control.

After World War II, the growing fears of the Cold War led the Soviets to almost completely seal Kyrgyzstan's borders so that new naval weapons could be tested in secret. Uranium was also secretly mined in the region.

INDEPENDENT KYRGYZSTAN

As the Soviet Union began to weaken in the 1980s, Kyrgyzstan remained the least politically organized of the Soviet Central Asian republics. Party politics were largely based on clan and regional loyalties.

Trouble developed over land and housing rights, rather than over political independence. A large area of land with an Uzbek majority had been attached to the Kyrgyz territory by the Stalinist government. In 1990, the Uzbeks, convinced that their land was being claimed for Kyrgyz housing, turned to violence. The ethnic conflict resulted in acts of brutality on both sides and claimed several hundred lives.

The Uzbek-Kyrgyz violence led many to blame the Communist Party leadership, and some felt the party should be disbanded. A compromise was struck by electing Askar Akayev president of the country's Supreme Soviet (the highest level of government) in October 1990. Forty-six-year-old Akayev was a respected physicist and the president of the Academy of Sciences. On August 31, 1991, the Kyrgyz Supreme Soviet voted for the declaration of independence, making Kyrgyzstan the first Central Asian republic to do so. A few weeks later, Akayev was re-elected as he ran unopposed in the full presidential election.

DIFFICULTIES AND DIVISIONS

During the first 10 years of independence, Kyrgyzstan faced severe economic difficulties. Between 1990 and 1997, industrial production dropped by 64 percent. Many Russian and German professionals left the country, creating a "brain drain" vacuum in their particular specialties. Ethnic divisions had characterized the labor force. Russians and Germans had dominated the technical and engineering professions, Uzbeks tended to work in the retail trade, and Kyrgyz largely held the bureaucratic, educational, agricultural, and cultural jobs. In addition, geographic divisions reflected unequal wealth, with the northern part of the country doing better economically than the impoverished south.

Kyrgyz leaders had trouble creating a sense of national unity. The mountains have isolated different parts of the country, and rural areas seem to have little in common with industrialized centers. Ethnic identities split along a north-south division, and President Akayev was a northerner.

AKAYEV RULES

In the beginning of his tenure as president, Akayev supported democracy and an independent media. He envisioned Kyrgyzstan as the "Switzerland of Central Asia" in an attempt to establish a national identity. However, the newly independent country had no previous history of independence—the heritage of the Kyrgystanis was of a pastoral nomadic culture. They didn't identify, in any deep sense, as a nation-state. To foster a sense of national unity, the year 2003 was celebrated as the 2,200th anniversary of Kyrgyz statehood, citing Chinese chronicles that showed a Kyrgyz state existed since the third century BCE.

Over the course of his presidency, Akayev's policies and tactics became more and more authoritarian. His early attempts to incorporate an open and inclusive government met with many obstacles. His political opponents, including former Communists as well as some of the *akims* (clan leaders), blocked many of his attempts at change. Meanwhile, the country's economy performed poorly during the radical transition from a Communist structure to a market-based structure, which added to popular discontent and mistrust of Akayev's reforms.

Frustrated and feeling threatened, Akayev increasingly began staffing his administration with friends, family, and other loyalists. He strengthened presidential powers and manipulated the constitutional court to allow him to run for a third term. He suppressed protests and dissidents, using criminal proceedings to silence his critics. State-controlled media outlets were biased in his favor, while independent media was pressured and journalists were intimidated. Corruption in high places was a common complaint.

In 2000, both the parliamentary elections and the presidential election were deemed by international observers to be not free and fair, marred by irregularities and allegations of fraud. Other complex issues also compelled the transition of Akayev from popular pro-democracy president to corrupt authoritarian leader.

TULIP REVOLUTION

By 2005, there were widespread calls for Akayev's resignation, particularly from the southern regions and the western cities. Matters came to a head following the parliamentary elections in February and early March, which were again deemed to be flawed. In what came to be called the Tulip Revolution, large anti-government demonstrations broke out in Jalal-Abad and Osh. Akayev refused to negotiate with protesters. Around 15,000 pro-opposition demonstrators took to the streets of Bishkek.

In a remarkable turn of events, Akayev and his family fled the country on March 24. That same day, the opposition produced detailed evidence of corruption throughout the Akayev family and administration. The president-in-exile went first to Kazakhstan and then to Russia, where the Russian president, Vladimir Putin, offered him exile. On April 4, 2005, Akayev resigned as Kyrgyzstan's president.

BAKIYEV TAKES OVER

The Tulip Revolution succeeded in sweeping Akayev and his administration from power. An interim government was formed with opposition leader Kurmanbek Bakiyev as prime minister. He, in turn, was elected president in a special election in July 2005. Foreign observers this time declared the election to be free and fair, but things did not go smoothly from there on out.

Demonstrations, such as this one in November 2006, have been commmon in Bishkek and other cities in Kyrgyzstan in the rocky period following independence.

Bakiyev had trouble establishing a stable government. In time, he began to be accused of the same things that had marred the previous administration—corruption, nepotism, intimidation of opposition candidates, and attacks on journalists. By 2007, protesters were demanding his resignation. Bakiyev was re-elected in 2009, although this time the fairness of the electoral process was questioned.

REVOLUTION #2

Meanwhile, the Kyrgyzstani people were experiencing power shortages and blackouts. Energy prices skyrocketed. A well-known Kyrgyz journalist, Gennady Pavluk (of Russian origin), was murdered. Other journalists were severely beaten. A rash of political killings reportedly followed the president's appointment of his brother as head of the National Security Guard.

In April 2010, history seemed to repeat itself as thousands of protesters attempted to storm the main government building in Bishkek. This time, riot police responded with live ammunition, killing around 80 people and wounding hundreds more. Protests quickly spread throughout the country, and the government declared a state of emergency. The following day, Bakiyev, like his predecessor, fled the capital. He eventually ended up in Belarus, where he was given refuge. Once again, an interim government took charge.

A NEW CONSTITUTION

Roza Otunbayeva, one of the key leaders of the Tulip Revolution, became Kyrgyzstan's head of the interim government. She held the post until a new election could take place, which occurred in 2011. Her short term was a time of ethnic violence between the Kyrgyz and Uzbeks in the Osh region—"the capital of the south." However, her government did accomplish a successful referendum on a new constitution, which was passed by a huge majority of voters.

The new constitution now prevents a president from seeking a second term. Since then, the country has had two more presidents, Almazbek Atambayev, from 2011 to 2017, and Sooronbay Jeenbekov since 2017. The next election is scheduled for 2023.

Both presidents' tenures have been anything but peaceful. Atambayev managed to alienate his own prime ministers (one of which was Jeenbekov, who would go on to succeed Atambayev as president) as well as other heads of state. Corruption remained pervasive, and antigovernment protests continued. Heavy-handed measures were used against political opponents and critics. In August 2019, the Jeenbekov government arrested the former president Atambayev following a dramatic standoff, charging him with corruption and a long list of other crimes.

INTERNET LINKS

https://www.advantour.com/kyrgyzstan/history.htm
This travel site gives a quick overview of Kyrgyzstan's history.

https://www.bbc.com/news/world-asia-16185772
BBC News presents a timeline of important events in the history of Kyrgyzstan.

https://jamestown.org/program/kyrgyz-regime-suspected-in-journalists-death
This article explains the possible Kyrgyzstani government complicity in a journalist's murder.

https://www.rferl.org/a/kyrgyz_presidents_chief_of_staff_says_bakiev_had_black_battalion/24357739.html
Radio Free Europe reports on President Bakiyev's alleged secret death squad.

GOVERNMENT

ДОМ СОЮЗОВ

A government building in Bishkek, built during the Soviet era, displays typical Soviet Communist motifs, such as the hammer and sickle at the top.

3

THE KYRGYZ REPUBLIC IS A parliamentary representative democratic republic. The president is the head of state, and the prime minister is the head of government. In this form of government, the people vote directly for the president. They vote for representatives in the legislature, or parliament, and the members of parliament then select the prime minister.

Although Kyrgyzstan is a predominantly Muslim nation, its government is secular, meaning separate from religious affiliation. This differs from many of the Muslim-majority nations of North Africa and the Persian Gulf region, which declare Islam to be the official national religion. The Kyrgyz Republic constitution ensures freedom of religion.

When Kyrgyzstan gained its independence in 1991, the country found itself mostly unprepared for both democracy and self-rule. For the previous 70 years, the nation had been controlled by the Soviet Union. The Soviets insisted that Kyrgyzstan had autonomy (independence), and its constitution seemed to guarantee that. In practice, however, every major decision was made in Moscow, the capital of the Soviet Union. This dominance extended beyond political matters to include the economy and the social and cultural life of the nation. The Kyrgyz Supreme Soviet, the highest governmental body in the republic, served little more than a ceremonial function.

The flag of Kyrgyzstan is red with a yellow sun in the center. The sun has 40 rays representing the 40 Kyrgyz tribes. In the center of the sun is a red ring crossed by two sets of three curving lines, a stylized representation of a *tunduk*–the crown or top of a traditional Kyrgyz yurt. The national colors are red and yellow, and the national symbol is a white falcon.

Another obstacle to establishing a working government was the lack of national unity. The nation's two major population centers—one in the north, the other in the south—were cut off from each other by mountains. In addition, people often felt greater loyalty to their family, clan, and region than to the rule of a national Kyrgyz government.

In spite of these stumbling blocks, the Kyrgyz set to work creating an independent and democratic government. However, the path has been rocky, with two revolutions in the 21st century, an ongoing problem with corruption, and a growing tendency toward authoritarian rule.

THE CONSTITUTION

In 2010, after Kyrgyzstan's second revolution succeeded in ousting President Kurmanbek Bakiyev, the country entered a new period of transition. During the short term of President Roza Otunbayeva, a new constitution was written. It was passed by referendum on June 27, 2010, replacing the 1993 version. Although it retained much of the original document, the new constitution strengthened the power of the parliament and reduced that of the president.

The document spells out human rights and freedoms in Kyrgyzstan. It declares men and women to "have equal rights and freedoms and equal opportunities for their realization." It prohibits discrimination "on the basis of sex, race, language, disability, ethnicity, belief, age, political and other convictions, education, background, proprietary and other status as well as other circumstances." In addition, the constitution bans slavery as well as the "death penalty, torture and other inhuman, cruel and degrading forms of treatment or punishment."

THE EXECUTIVE BRANCH

Under the new constitution, the president serves a single six-year term. He or she cannot be re-elected. Although presidential power is weaker under the new arrangement, the position is not merely ceremonial, as is often the case in parliamentary systems. The president has veto power and the ability to appoint certain officials. The next presidential election is to be held in 2023.

The prime minister is nominated by the majority party or majority coalition in parliament. Upon parliamentary approval, he or she is appointed by the president.

THE LEGISLATIVE BRANCH

The Kyrgyzstani parliament is a unicameral (one-house) body called the Jogorku Kengest ("Supreme Council"). This legislature is the government entity that makes the laws. It is made up of 120 seats, with members being directly elected in a national election. Political parties put forth lists of candidates; voters then vote for the party of their choice. Winning candidates are then seated according to the proportional representation vote. Members serve five-year terms. The next elections are scheduled for 2025.

The constitution limits any single political party to a maximum of 65 of the parliament's 120 seats. This prevents any party from accruing too much power. In addition, political parties may not be founded on ethnic or religious grounds, and members of the police, armed forces, and judiciary are prohibited from joining parties.

The Freedom Monument (*left*) is a focal point of Ala-Too Square, the municipal and governmental center of Bishkek.

The preamble to the constitution of the Kyrgyz Republic states that its mission is "to build a free and democratic state based on respect and protection of human rights." Any country may call itself a democracy, but how well does the description fit the reality? In some cases, there's quite a wide gap between the high-minded words in a nation's constitution and the actuality. It all depends on how well a government functions to protect democratic principles.

Several international organizations watch closely to evaluate how well the world's governments are doing on that score.

Freedom House is a U.S.-based independent watchdog organization that conducts research and advocacy on democracy, political freedom, and human rights. In its annual Freedom in the World report, it ranks nations on such matters and assigns a finding of "Free," "Partly Free," or "Not Free."

In its 2019 report, it expressed concern about freedom in Kyrgyzstan, ranking it "Partly Free" with an aggregate score of 38 out of 100. For comparison, the United States ranked 86th, earning the rank of "Free." Finland, Norway, and Sweden all earned a perfect score of 100, with Syria coming in last with a "Not Free" score of 0.

The report noted that, in Kyrgyzstan, "political parties are primarily vehicles for a handful of strong personalities, rather than mass organizations with clear ideologies and policy platforms." It noted that the government continues to be unstable: "The prime minister has been replaced nearly a dozen times since 2010." The report also points to fraudulent or questionable elections; rampant corruption, including widespread corruption among judges; discrimination and violence against Uzbeks; and intimidation and suppression of political opponents, human rights activists, and journalists.

THE JUDICIAL BRANCH

The judicial branch, or court system, administers justice according to the law, beginning with the local courts and working up to the Supreme Court, which is the court of final appeal. This highest-level court also determines the constitutionality of laws, a task that was once the domain of the Constitutional Court. However, the 2010 constitution did away with the Constitutional Court and transferred its powers and duties to the Constitutional Chamber of the Supreme Court.

The Supreme Court consists of 25 judges, whose necessary qualifications are spelled out in the constitution. The Constitutional Chamber of the Supreme Court consists of the chairperson, deputy chairperson, and nine judges. The Supreme Court judges are appointed by the parliament on the recommendation of the president. Those judges serve for 10 years; Constitutional Chamber judges serve for 15 years, but in both cases, the mandatory retirement age is 70.

LOCAL GOVERNMENT

The country is divided into seven provinces, called oblasts, along with the cities of Bishtek and Osh. Among these, there are 40 administrative districts called rayons, which are further divided and run by city, town, and village councils.

INTERNET LINKS

https://www.cia.gov/library/publications/the-world-factbook/geos/kg.html
The World Factbook provides up-to-date information about the government of Kyrgyzstan.

https://www.constituteproject.org/constitution/Kyrgyz_Republic_2010.pdf
This is a transcript of the 2010 constitution of the Kyrgyz Republic.

https://freedomhouse.org/country/kyrgyzstan
Freedom House annually assesses the country's status of political rights and civil liberties.

https://www.worldatlas.com/articles/what-type-of-government-does-kyrgyzstan-have.html
This site provides a short overview of the structure of government in the Kyrgyz Republic.

ECONOMY

A farmer uses a horse-drawn tool to rake dry grasses on the Suusamyr plateau, a remote region about 8,200 feet (2,500 m) above sea level.

4

BEFORE THE OUTBREAK OF THE global COVID-19 pandemic in early 2020, Kyrgyzstan's economy was growing slowly. In 2019, the country's economy had grown by 6.1 percent in the first three quarters of the year, which is an impressive number in the world of economic growth. However, experts point out that on closer look, the number isn't as great as it seems, and the nation's economy had really only been slugging along at a lackluster rate.

Kyrgyzstan's economic development has been hampered by corruption, government instability, a lack of diversity in its industries—overreliance on a single gold mine—and difficulty attracting foreign aid and investment. Wages remain low, on average a little less than $250 per month in 2020. In 2015, about one-third of the population was estimated to be living below the poverty line. (Poverty line estimations differ from country to country and are inexact at best. Nevertheless, this would be a fairly high rate of poverty in any accounting.)

The pandemic outbreak caused the economic picture to deteriorate rapidly. The government closed its borders with China, the source of more than one-third of all of its merchandise imports. It also implemented border restrictions with Kazakhstan and Uzbekistan, all of which hindered economic activity. It's too soon, at this writing, to predict what the effect of the pandemic will have on Kyrgyzstan's economy in the long run, but in the immediate future, growth is sure to slow markedly.

THE OLD ECONOMY

For most of the 20th century, Kyrgyzstan functioned much like a colony serving the Soviet Union. Kyrgyz farms and mines provided agricultural products and raw materials that were shipped to other parts of the Soviet Union. The country was totally dependent on Moscow for planning, trade, investment, and technology. Most of the consumer products people used were purchased from the Soviet Union, including items made from Kyrgyz raw materials.

When the republic gained independence in 1991, the Kyrgyz people and government began developing both a democracy and a free-market (capitalist) economy. Major economic and social measures were passed in order to shift from a Communist-planned economy to a free-market system that relied on the forces of demand and supply.

A group of people sing a pro-Communist song at a rally on May 1, the international Labor Day, in Bishkek. Some older people think life was better under Soviet rule.

Gross domestic product (GDP) is a measure of a country's total production. The number reflects the total value of goods and services produced over one year. Economists use it to determine whether a country's economy is growing or contracting. Growth is good, while a falling GDP means trouble. Dividing the GDP by the number of people in the country determines the GDP per capita (per person). This number provides an indication of a country's average standard of living—the higher the better.

In 2017, the GDP per capita (adjusted to purchasing power parity) in Kyrgyzstan was approximately $3,700. The 2017 figure is considered quite low, and it ranked Kyrgyzstan 183rd out of 228 countries listed by the CIA World Factbook. *For comparison, the United States that year was number 19, with a GDP per capita of $59,500. Kyrgyzstan's neighbor Uzbekistan was ranked 158th, with a per capita GDP of $6,900. Turkmenistan was at number 97 with $18,200, and Kazakhstan was better still at 79, with $26,300.*

THE TRANSITION STRUGGLE

During the 1990s, the Kyrgyz lived through tremendous economic upheaval. Subsidies supplied by Moscow, which had provided 53 percent of the national budget, disappeared. By 1995, agricultural output fell by 84 percent, and industrial production dropped 64 percent. Inflation soared, hitting the incredible figure of 1,300 percent in 1993, before falling to 300 percent the following year.

By the mid-1990s, people's hopes surged as the new economy began to show healthy improvement, with industrial output up 35 percent and agricultural production up more than 10 percent. Foreign investors showed interest, including a Canadian company that formed a partnership to open the Kumtor gold mine.

In 1998, the bubble of prosperity burst when Kyrgyzstan's three major trade partners—Russia, Uzbekistan, and Kazakhstan—faced severe financial crises of their own. The result was a sharp decline in Kyrgyzstan's growth. By 2002, Kyrgyzstan's gross domestic product (GDP) had reached only 66 percent of what it had been before independence.

Another problem that emerged during the transition years was a major loss of talented and qualified personnel, as foreign workers decided to go back to their home countries. As many as 250 left every day, primarily Russians and Germans, who took their skills and knowledge of technology and various scientific fields with them. There was no quick way for the country to fill this gap in expertise.

Meanwhile, Kyrgyzstani workers went abroad to find work and send money home. This practice is still common and accounts for a good segment of the county's economy. Remittances (money sent home) from Kyrgyzstani migrant workers, mostly laboring in Russia and Kazakhstan, are equivalent to more than one-quarter of Kyrgyzstan's GDP.

AGRICULTURE

Almost half of Kyrgyzstan's labor force works in agriculture. Only 6.7 percent of the total land area is used for crop cultivation—major crops include cotton,

A woman bags potatoes at a weekend farmers' market near Victory Square in Bishkek.

A man grooms an animal at a cattle market in Tokmok in the Chuy Region, or Province, of Kyrgyzstan.

potatoes, vegetables, grapes, and other fruits and berries. Farmers also grow grasses, grains, and other crops for animal fodder; and wheat, barley, corn, and rice for human consumption. Farming is best suited for the Fergana Valley; the Chuy Province, which contains the rich, flat soil of the Chu River Valley; and the Talas Province, with its Talas River Valley. Even so, many farms require irrigation. In 2012, about 3,951 square miles (10,233 sq km) of land were irrigated.

A greater segment of the agricultural sector is devoted to animal husbandry. Around 48.3 percent of the land is used as pastures for livestock, and raising animals is the livelihood of many of the country's rural people. Cattle, sheep, goats, and horses provide milk and meat. The mountainous regions lend themselves best to this sort of use, as animals can graze on high, grassy

Horses graze on a high *jailoo* near Song Kul Lake.

pastures. It's also a good fit for nomadic lifestyles, as families can follow their herds to the *jailoo*, or remote summer pastures, where they can live in their yurts.

One problem facing this way of life, however, is the degradation of the lower-altitude winter pasturelands from overgrazing. Part of the trouble is that the higher pasturelands have become less accessible, as Soviet-era bridges and roads have fallen apart and become unusable. Sustainable land use practices to restore a healthy balance to this sector will require investment.

Despite the large numbers of people working in agriculture, the sector accounts for less than 15 percent of the total GDP. Mainly, this is because most farms are small, subsistence operations—meaning the farmers grow only enough for their own use. Increasing production will require modernizing farming methods, which in turn requires financial support and education.

INDUSTRY AND MINING

During the Soviet period, the Russians introduced the manufacture of high-technology electronic parts. The plants in Kyrgyzstan relied on supplies from other republics and skilled technicians from Russia and Germany. Some factories producing mostly household products were also set up.

When the Soviet Union crumbled, so did Kyrgyzstan's fledgling industries. The market for Kyrgyz goods collapsed, factories closed their doors, and the nation lost its pool of skilled foreign workers.

Manufacturing has made somewhat of a comeback, particularly in textiles and clothing and food processing. The garment industry accounts for about 7 percent of the country's total exports, and it employs about 300,000 workers.

Mining is crucial to Kyrgyzstan's economy. Among its natural resources are coal, iron ore, aluminum, copper, silver, mercury, and other minerals. However, much depends on the output of just one single gold mine—the Kumtor mine in the Issyk-Kul Region accounts for about 10 percent of the country's GDP, according to the World Bank.

Workers operate sewing machines at a garment factory in Bishkek.

In 1978, a rich deposit of gold was discovered in Kyrgyzstan's Issyk-Kul Region in the east. It took a while, but by 1997, the hills were finally yielding up their treasure as the Canadian Centerra Gold mining company began production there. The mine is located around 217 miles (350 km) southeast of the capital Bishkek and around 37 miles (60 km) north of the border with China.

In 2019, the facility produced 600,000 ounces of gold, or about three-quarters of the company's entire yield. Centerra also has mines in Canada and Turkey. Although Centerra Gold is Canadian, the Kyrgyz Republic is its largest shareholder, holding around 26 percent of its shares.

Kumtor is an open pit mine. This technique of extracting minerals from the earth involves digging an open pit of terraced levels, using drill, blast, shovel, and truck methods. The pit is enlarged until the mineral source—in this case, gold—is exhausted. Open-pit mining is one of the most dangerous sectors in the industrial world. It is also one of the most ecologically damaging. Toxic waste products are released into the air and often flow into waterways. When abandoned, the stripped earth is left a barren wasteland.

Located around 2.8 miles (4.5 km) above sea level, Kumtor is the second-highest gold mining operation in the world. It's also in a region of large, active glaciers. Accessing its ore is difficult, expensive, and dangerous. Over the past few years, Kumtor has been the scene of a number of fatal accidents, one of which led to a criminal investigation into Centerra. In December 2019, two workers were killed when a landslide buried their trucks.

HYDROELECTRIC POWER

While other Central Asian countries have large reserves of oil that major powers are eager to develop, Kyrgyzstan's most valuable resource is water. Although landlocked, the mountainous country's glaciers, snowfields, and rivers make up one of the world's great sources of fresh water. The country generates 80 to 90 percent of its electricity from 6 hydroelectric plants—all located on the Naryn River. The rest of its energy needs are met with fossil fuels. The country operates no nuclear power plants. (Nevertheless, the town of Mailuu-Suu is one of several sites that have been polluted by radioactive waste from Soviet-era uranium mines.)

Kyrgyzstan's hydroelectric potential, however, is far from realized. Experts estimate the country is using only 10 percent of its possible hydropower energy resources, and many of its existing power plants are old and outdated. Additionally, the country has other potential renewable sources—such as solar, wind, and biomass—that are still largely untapped. In recent years, the government of the Kyrgyz Republic has been implementing various reforms, programs, and projects in the energy sector aimed at improving energy facilities.

The Toktogul Dam and hydroelectric power station opened in 1976. It is on the Naryn River in the Jalal-Abad Province of Kyrgyzstan.

TOURISM

With its amazing variety of breathtaking landscapes and ecosystems, Kyrgyzstan should be a tourist paradise. Its magnificent mountains rival any peaks on earth. The country's cultural and historical heritage, with its exotic Silk Road connections, only adds to its potential to lure visitors from afar. So far, though, tourism makes up a fairly small piece of the economy. In 2016,

Tourists smear mud over their bodies in Issyk-Kul Salt Lake. The mud is thought to have healing properties.

the tourism industry accounted for an estimated 3.9 percent of the national GDP. It employed about 3.7 percent of the labor force.

In 2017, around 3,309,400 visitors came to Kyrgyzstan. That was a 12.9 percent uptick from the year before in a trend that was generally rising since a low in 2010. (Note: The coronavirus pandemic will drastically affect the totals for 2020.) Tourism has grown slowly because of a lack of investment. Although some tourists—the backpacking set—enjoy adventure travel with no amenities, they are not in the majority. To attract the usual international tourists, hotels, restaurants, transportation systems, and even medical facilities need to be built and improved.

Ecotourism is a growing field of interest and one that lends itself to Kyrgyzstanis' unusual lifestyle. Community-based tourism offers tourists the chance to stay with Kyrgyz families and even to travel on horseback or in four-wheel-drive vehicles through mountain and highland regions. Travelers eat with the locals, following their traditional diet, and sleep in yurts among the herds of sheep, horses, and goats.

Tourism also brings in customers for native artisans making traditional handicrafts, especially the carpets called *shyrdaks*. Produced in homes or in local co-ops, these handicrafts help build local economies.

INTERNET LINKS

https://eurasianet.org/kyrgyzstans-farming-puzzle-a-rich-nation-reliant-on-others
This article examines some of the difficulties facing Kyrgyzstani farmers.

https://www.kumtor.kg/en
This is the home site of Centerra Gold's Kumtor mining operation.

https://ourworld.unu.edu/en/pastures-for-the-future
This site features an article and video about the life of a Kyrgyzstani herding family.

https://www.worldatlas.com/articles/what-are-the-biggest-industries-in-kyrgyzstan.html
This site gives a good overview of Kyrgyzstan's economy.

ENVIRONMENT

One of the few snow leopards left in Kyrgyzstan is protected in a conservation reserve.

5

THE RUGGED MOUNTAINS OF Kyrgyzstan, which cover nine-tenths of the nation, give the country its stunning natural beauty. However, the harsh terrain also means that many plants and animals are confined to small, often fragile habitats. There are 20 different ecosystems in the country, from deserts, steppes, and alpine mountains to walnut forests and wetlands.

A relatively minor change in temperature or precipitation can reduce a species' chance of survival and set it dangerously on the road to extinction. For example, climate change has caused the glaciers of this high-altitude nation to recede by 20 percent. There is great concern that they could disappear altogether by 2100, if not sooner.

The environment also faces other serious problems, largely caused by humans. Many of these are the result of more than 70 years of mismanagement by Soviet planners. In addition, some difficulties have resulted simply from the increased population density in the region. Over the past century, for example, Kyrgyzstan has lost about half its forests, which covered only a small part of the country to begin with. Much of the loss has been the result of poor timber management. Damage also occurred during the hard times of the 1990s, when people cut down acres of trees for fuel.

Snow leopards are large cats native to the Tian Shan and other mountain ranges of Central Asia and South Asia. The animals have whitish fur with black spots and rosettes. They usually live at high altitudes in rocky terrain, where their broad paws help them walk on snow. The greatest threat to snow leopards has been hunting for their skins and body parts. Climate change may also threaten their population by reducing their habitat.

Plastic trash piles up on a river bank in Kant, a town in the Chuy Valley of northern Kyrgyzstan.

POLLUTION

Looking at photographs of pristine mountain vistas, it can be hard to believe that pollution is a problem in such a remote land, but it is. Air pollution is a serious side effect of industrial output; crowded urban areas where there are many old, poorly maintained vehicles on the roads; and the use of coal in power plants and low-grade fuels in homes.

Water pollution is a result of industrial and agricultural runoff, as well as improper treatment of household wastewater. Household waste (trash) is far from adequately managed. The mining industry leaches toxic substances into the soils and waterways. In one notorious mining accident at the Kumtor gold mine in 1998, a truck spilled nearly 2 tons (1.8 metric tons) of sodium cyanide into the Barskoon River. The spill occurred about 5 miles (8 km) upstream from the village of Barskoon, where residents use the river water for drinking and for irrigating their crops. The mining company waited six to eight hours before reporting the situation to the local authorities. In the aftermath, the spill left several people dead and hundreds seeking medical treatment, and thousands of others evacuated from their homes. Villagers, seeking compensation, filed lawsuits that continued on for years.

Over the past few years, the Kyrgyz government has become increasingly committed to environmental protection. In addition, several environmental groups have been formed and work in cooperation with United Nations (UN) agencies.

THE SOVIET LEGACY

During the years of Communist rule in the Soviet Union, all major decisions were made in Moscow. As Soviet bureaucrats worked out their various plans to develop their holdings, protecting the environment was not a top priority. Instead, the planners thought in terms of taming the environment, forcing it to yield the resources the Communist empire needed.

Just as the radical shift to full-force cotton production took its toll on the land, so did the damming of rivers in order to increase irrigation. A good example is provided by the Aral Sea, an inland sea between Uzbekistan and Kazakhstan. Changing the course of rivers that flow into the Aral Sea has been rapidly lowering their water levels, leaving fishing villages that were once onshore stranded many miles from the water. Although this environmental disaster affects Uzbekistan and Kazakhstan more directly, the tragedy provides a lesson for all of Central Asia: Of the 173 animal species once found around the sea, only 38 remain. The rest have moved away or died out.

The overgrazing of pastureland was another legacy of the Soviet years. Between 1941 and 1991, there was a determined effort to increase Kyrgyzstan's livestock. While sheep and goat populations increased in all the Soviet republics, the numbers quadrupled in Kyrgyzstan to 10 million animals. Although the numbers have since been reduced to more manageable flock sizes, the overgrazing that resulted from such massive herds produced serious erosion. Today, the total pastureland in the country has been reduced by one-third, and an estimated 70 percent of the remaining grassland still suffers from the effects of erosion.

The needs of the Soviet military also added to the environmental damage. The testing of top-secret weapons was conducted in Kyrgyzstan, especially during the Cold War years of the 1950s and 1960s, and large-scale mining for uranium in the Tian Shan mountains was continued into the 1980s. As many as 50 abandoned mine sites may now still be leaking radioactive substances or contaminating groundwater.

ENDANGERED SPECIES

In the 21st century, the endangered species of Kyrgyzstan include 53 species of birds, 26 species of mammals, 2 species of amphibians, 8 species of reptiles, 7 species of fish, 18 species of arthropods, 89 species of higher plants, and

Dholes historically roamed Central Asia but are thought to be extinct in Kyrgyzstan.

6 species of fungi. As a consequence of human activity, some species have disappeared completely, including 3 species of large or medium-sized mammals.

The Caspian tiger once lived in Kyrgyzstan and other parts of Central Asia and Siberia. Since the 1970s, however, it has been extinct, both in the wild and in captivity. Habitat destruction, hunting, and targeted extermination to protect livestock all led to the extinction. There are currently no tigers of any species living in the wild in Kyrgyzstan.

The dhole is a foxlike creature also called a red dog, whistling dog, or Indian wild dog. The Tian Shan dhole is a subspecies native to the Tian Shan and Altai mountain ranges and was once widespread in Kyrgyzstan and other parts of Central Asia. Today, however, it may be completely gone from the country, though a few Tian Shan dholes still live in Tibet and parts of northwestern China.

The snow leopard, the last of the big cats to make its home in Kyrgyzstan, is still seen in the higher mountain elevations, but its numbers have diminished rapidly. It is believed that 4,000 to 7,000 remain worldwide. Because the value of a single snow leopard's skin is many times that of the minimum annual wage, the animal is in high demand among poachers.

According to the international environmental organization NABU (German Society for Nature Conservation), which operates a rehabilitation center in Kyrgyzstan, there are only around 260 snow leopards left in the entire country. The population has fallen by almost 80 percent in only a few years due to poaching and illegal trade.

Overhunting and poaching are placing other species in danger. Poaching is hard to stop, especially in difficult economic times, because it is one way for rural villagers to earn money. Nonetheless the impact can be devastating on some species. The saiga antelope is killed for its horns, for example, which are sold to Chinese medicine makers. Similarly, musk deer are killed for their musk glands, which are used in perfumes. It takes 160 deer to produce about 2 pounds (0.9 kg) of musk, so it is no surprise that the musk deer population has declined dramatically.

LICENSE TO KILL

There are now 10 nature preserves, 13 national parks, and many other protected areas in Kyrgyzstan, covering around 7.4 percent of the country's total area. However, far more of the country—70 percent—is open to hunting concessions. Many international trophy hunting companies sponsor excursions to Kyrgyzstan to hunt large animals, such as the ibex. This has resulted in a sharp decline in the population of some species. With ibex and argali sheep—a large wild sheep of Central Asia—being important prey for the snow leopard, a reduction in their herds is having the secondary effect of a decline in the leopard populations. When more animals are killed than can naturally reproduce, as is the case with those species, the result is naturally a plummet to extinction.

Until recently, a license to kill a Marco Polo sheep—a subspecies of argali sheep and Kyrgyzstan's most prized trophy—was $3,600. A Siberian ibex

Hunting in Kyrgyzstan has put some species at risk of dying out.

could be shot for just $500. The fees have almost doubled in recent years yet are still sufficiently competitive in the international market. Kyrgyzstan does not prohibit the hunting of rare, threatened, or endangered species; it merely charges more for the licenses. Even then, its enforcement is quite lax.

A bill to enact a complete ban on hunting until 2030 was put before Kyrgyzstan's parliament in 2017. It was narrowly defeated, 56—52, but it did spark a passionate debate over the environmental sustainability of the hunting industry.

PROTECTED LANDS

One former trophy hunting concession in Kyrgyzstan was turned into a wildlife sanctuary. Shamshy, in the northern Tian Shan mountains, is home to Siberian ibex, argali sheep, and wolves, and lies within a large snow leopard territory. Hunting is banned, and it's hoped that the ibex and sheep will thrive there. In turn, the sanctuary might attract more snow leopards.

Some protected areas, such as the Sary-Chelek Biosphere Reserve, are operated in collaboration with a development agency of the European Union (EU) and with the United Nations (UN). Sary-Chelek, covering the entire southern side of the Chatkal mountain range, provides habitats for more than one-third of the country's plant and animal species. Poaching has been a serious problem, because people living in the region have cut down trees and harvested nuts, berries, other fruits, and honey, especially during the 1990s when the economy was gripped by a depression. To reduce poaching, authorities are now offering alternatives, such as grants to establish tourist-related businesses.

Near Sary-Chelek is the Besh Aral Biosphere Reserve. Like Sary-Chelek, this is a region of exceptional natural beauty as well as a home to many rare plant and animal species. Besh Aral, operated in collaboration with other Central Asian countries as well as with the UN and the EU, includes parts of Uzbekistan and Kazakhstan. The reserve staff provides education, training, and financial aid for local populations, while also overseeing the use of pastures and forests.

The largest reserve, the Sarychat Ertash State Nature Reserve, covers 331,467 acres (134,140 ha) in the Issyk-Kul Region. It was founded in 1995 mainly to protect the endangered snow leopard and the argali sheep. Other large

The Ramsar Convention on Wetlands is an international treaty for the conservation and sustainable use of wetlands. The treaty dates to 1971 and is named for the Iranian city of Ramsar, where it was signed. The convention uses a broad definition of wetlands—it includes all lakes and rivers, underground aquifers, swamps and marshes, wet grasslands, peatlands, oases, estuaries, deltas and tidal flats, mangroves and other coastal areas, coral reefs, and all human-made sites such as fish ponds, rice paddies, reservoirs, and salt pans.

Wetlands are of vital importance, according to the convention, because they are among the world's most productive environments. They are ecosystems of "biological diversity that provide the water and productivity upon which countless species of plants and animals depend for survival."

As part of its mission, the convention identifies wetlands sites around the world that are of international importance and works to protect them. Of the 2,390 Ramsar sites (as of 2020), Kyrgyzstan has three, with a combined surface area of 1,678,854 acres

(679,408 hectares). These are the Issyk-Kul State Nature Reserve with Lake Issyk-Kul; Song Kul Lake, a large high-altitude freshwater lake in central Kyrgyzstan; and Chatyr Kul, a saline high-altitude lake in the Tian Shan mountains.

mammals in this reserve are the Siberian ibex, wild boar, Eurasian lynx, Eurasian wolf, and Eurasian brown bear. This reserve is strictly off-limits to the public.

In 2000, the Issyk-Kul Biosphere Reserve was established to protect the ecosystems of the region. It is one of the UNESCO World Network of Biosphere Reserves. The plan for this reserve includes controlled land use for farming and herding, as well as community-based tourism. Lake Issyk-Kul itself is a Ramsar site of globally significant biodiversity.

INTERNET LINKS

https://www.aljazeera.com/news/2019/11/kyrgyzstan-wildlife-bounces-hunting-moratorium-191103060713037.html
This video focuses on the country's efforts to protect wildlife, especially snow leopards.

https://www.nationalgeographic.com/news/2016/06/snow-leopards-conservation-kyrgyzstan/#close
This article discusses the plight of snow leopards in Kyrgyzstan.

https://rsis.ramsar.org/sites/default/files/rsiswp_search/exports/Ramsar-Sites-annotated-summary-Kyrgyzstan.pdf?1589039996
This page describes the three Ramsar sites in Kyrgyzstan.

https://www.snowleopard.org/a-first-glimpse-at-the-wildlife-of-shamshy-sanctuary
https://www.snowleopard.org/from-hunting-reserve-to-wildlife-sanctuary
https://www.snowleopard.org/snow-leopard-facts
These pages provide information, maps, and photos about snow leopards and the Shamshy Sanctuary.

KYRGYZSTANIS

This man is wearing an *ak-kalpak*, the traditional national hat of Kyrgyzstan.

6

T HE CITIZENS OF KYRGYZSTAN ARE called Kyrgyzstanis. Many of them, but not all, are also Kyrgyz. Kyrgyzstani is a national description; Kyrgyz is an ethnic one. Sometimes, all people in the country are refered to as Kyrgyz—probably because Kyrgyzstani is a long word— but technically, there is a difference.

Nearly three-quarters of the population, about 73.5 percent, is ethnically Kyrgyz. Uzbeks are the second-largest ethnic group, making up 14.7 percent. Around 5.5 percent of Kyrgyzstanis are ethnic Russians, and the rest are Dungan, Uigher, Tajik, Turk, Kazakh, Tatar, Ukrainian, Korean, or German.

Around 72 million people live in Central Asia, in one of five independent republics. Uzbekistan is the most populous country, with about 33 million people. Kazakhstan is by far the largest in terms of area but has only 18 million people. Tajikistan is the smallest in area but has 9 million people. Kyrgyzstan has about 6.5 million people, and Turkmenistan, the most sparsely populated, has about 5.6 million people.

More than 80 national and ethnic groups are scattered throughout the region. The ebb and flow of peoples across the continent for more than 20 centuries created the mix that is modern-day Kyrgyzstan. In addition, the Soviet system of drawing national boundaries left groups of one nationality residing inside another country, such as the Uzbeks who now live within the borders of Kyrgyzstan.

There are several theories as to the origin of the name *Kyrgyz*. The most common theory is that the term derives from the Turkic word *kyrk* ("forty") and *yz* ("tribes"), meaning "a collection of 40 tribes." Those would be the 40 clans originally united by the legendary hero Manas in the country's origin myth. The Persian suffix *stan* means "country" or "land," so *Kyrgyzstan* means "Land of the Kyrgyz."

Shepherds on horseback drive their herds across the high mountain pastures near Lake Song Kul in Kyrgyzstan.

THE KYRGYZ

The people who are currently known as the Kyrgyz make up one of the oldest ethnic groups recorded in Asia, first mentioned in the second century BCE. Described in ancient Chinese sources as a fair-skinned people with green eyes and reddish hair, they were said to have a mix of European and East Asian features. They lived in a loose confederation of tribes in Siberia. Beginning in the ninth century, they started moving south into Central Asia. Some migrated to present-day Kyrgyzstan to get away from wars, and thousands came as soldiers in the Mongol armies of Genghis Khan.

By the time these migrations ended in the 1500s, the Kyrgyz had formed a solid majority in the area that became Kyrgyzstan. (Smaller communities of them ended up in other regions throughout Central Asia and even in Turkey.) They lived primarily as nomadic herders, raising Asian fat-tailed sheep, goats, Bactrian camels, and horses. Those hardy horses, a breed called Kazakh horses, came to be a great source of individual wealth. They provided meat and *kymyz*, an important beverage made of fermented mare's milk. The horses and camels were also used for transporting goods along the Silk Road.

A Kyrgyz's identity and place in society depends in large part on his or her tribal and regional origins. Today, the Kyrgyz are divided into roughly 30 tribes, or *sanjiras*, and the tribes are clustered into two regional groups. The groups are quite distinct, and they are in constant competition for political power and influence. One group consists of the northerners, or Tagai, who also include Kyrgyz who are living in Kazakhstan. The southerners, or Ich Kilik, include Kyrgyz living in Tajikistan and China.

The northern tribes include the Sary Bagysh, which is the tribe of the former president Akayev and those closest to him. These northern tribes have lived with Russian settlers for several generations and tend to be more like the Russians than Kyrgyz who settled in other parts of the country. The southern tribes, through greater contact with Uzbeks, have adopted a more devout approach to Islam. The northern and southern groups have also developed some language differences to the extent that they can sometimes have difficulty communicating.

These tribal and regional networks continue to be important. Although the government hopes to reduce the influence of the tribes, they continue to provide the path to political appointments. Connections gained through them can also be critical in getting a job or promotion, even in obtaining a better booth for one's wares at a bazaar.

DWINDLING MINORITIES

The breakup of the Soviet Union led to confusing shifts in population throughout Europe and Asia beginning in 1990 and 1991. Many Russians left Kyrgyzstan to return to their native country in order to take part in the rebuilding of their homeland. The same was true of other national minorities—the Ukrainians, Georgians, and East Germans.

Later in the decade, ethnic tension and conflict caused more migrations. Russians in particular felt that they were being pushed out by being denied opportunities for jobs and government appointments, even though there had been many Russians in the country for 150 years. Between 1989 and 1999, an estimated 273,000 Russians left Kyrgyzstan, reducing the Russian population by one-third.

The same feeling of exclusion led many Germans to leave, reducing their numbers by 61,000, which represented nearly 80 percent of that minority. Similarly, around 36,000 Ukrainians left—roughly half of their former population in Kyrgyzstan.

OTHER MINORITIES

Uzbeks are the largest minority group in Kyrgyzstan, representing about 14.7 percent of the population. Most live in and around the Fergana Valley, which is a natural geographical extension of Uzbekistan. Uzbeks have traditionally supported themselves through farming and trading. Their lifestyle and their deep devotion to Islam set them apart from their Kyrgyz neighbors.

The boundary area between Uzbekistan and Kyrgyzstan has erupted in violence several times since independence. In addition to the ethnic fighting of the early 1990s, in 1999 and 2000 the extremist Islamic Movement of Uzbekistan (IMU) launched a series of raids across the border, occupying towns and taking hostages. After Kyrgyz troops drove them out, the Uzbek government decided to plant land mines along the border between the two countries. It is thought that key IMU leaders were killed when the United States invaded Afghanistan in 2002, prompting the IMU to stop its aggressive actions.

The Uighurs (or Uyghurs) are a smaller group, making up only about 1 percent of the population of Kyrgyzstan. They are related to the Uzbeks and are also farmers and traders. Most Uighurs live near cities such as Bishkek and Osh.

Several other Central Asian ethnic groups are represented in the country's population. Tatars, Kazakhs, Tajiks, and Turks combined make up only about 2 percent of the population, but they add rich variety to Kyrgyzstani life.

Villages around Bishkek, and in the capital city itself, are home to two small but growing groups, Dungans and Koreans. The Dungans are Chinese Muslims. The Koreans lived around Vladivostok in the Soviet Union until World War II, when Joseph Stalin, fearing that they might be spies for the Japanese, had them deported.

Both groups worked hard to establish themselves. Some worked in specialized agriculture, while others entered technical professions such as electronics. Today, Dungans and Koreans are among the most prosperous people in Kyrgyzstan.

INTERNET LINKS

https://data.unicef.org/country/kgz
UNICEF has demographic statistics for Kyrgyzstan.

https://www.thecrowdedplanet.com/dungan-people-kyrgyzstan-cuisine
This photo essay focuses on the Dungan people in Kyrgyzstan.

https://www.trtworld.com/magazine/how-the-dungan-community-protects-its-identity-from-regional-influences-20200
This article looks at the experience of the Dungan people of Kyrgyzstan.

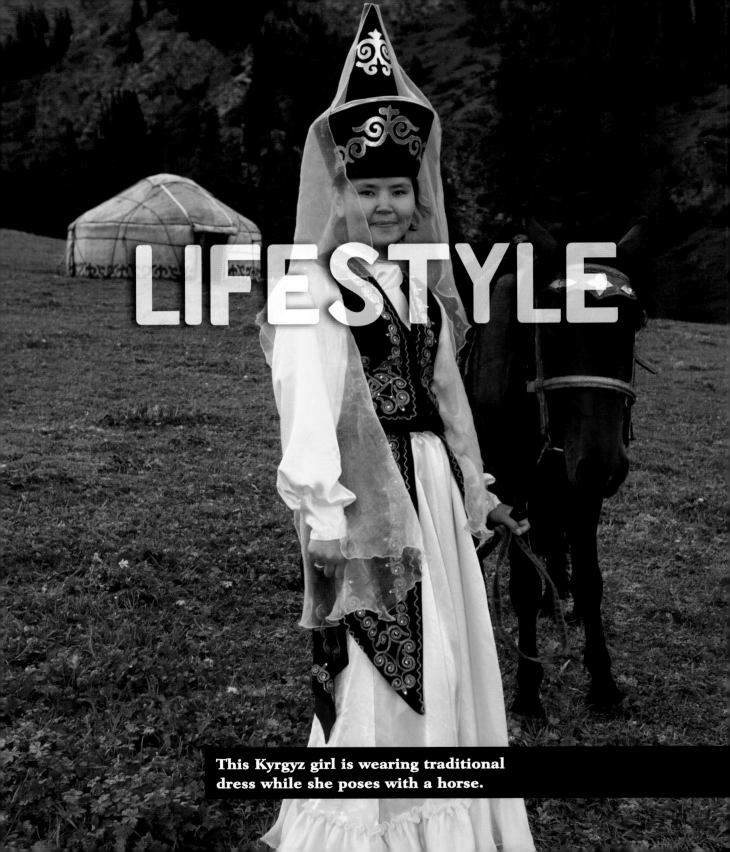

LIFESTYLE

This Kyrgyz girl is wearing traditional dress while she poses with a horse.

7

MOST KYRGYZSTANIS LIVE RURAL lifestyles. Nearly two-thirds of the population can be found in the country's abundant mountains, grassy steppes, and river valleys that formed their history as a nomadic people.

That history still deeply influences their lifestyle today. Hospitality, for example, is of great importance. Any stranger is always welcome to share another's home and food. If a family lives in poverty, the members will still give all they can to their guests. This kind of hospitality helped people survive in the almost lawless days of the Silk Road, when travelers had to rely on the goodwill of those they encountered.

While friendly to strangers, Kyrgyz are often distrustful of people in authority. In their nomadic life, the people relied on their village elders and their tribal leader. This clan loyalty still dominates in many areas, where people feel more kinship to their local group than to the nation as a whole.

In the 20th century, Soviet authorities actively tried to disrupt that tradition and instill a patriotic obedience to Moscow. The Kyrgyz response was to appear to be obeying Soviet authority while secretly maintaining their own traditional lifestyle. By living this kind of dual existence, they managed to preserve a great deal of their traditional culture.

CITY LIFE

Even a predominantly rural nation has its cities, and Kyrgyzstan is no exception. About 37 percent of the population lives in urban areas, a trend

Furniture is a Western idea that Kyrgyzstanis adopted during Soviet times. After all, furniture was not conducive to nomadic lifestyles. Today, northerners may have a table and chairs for meals, but southerners will spread a *dastarkon* (tablecloth) directly on the floor and sit on soft mats. Throughout the country, floors and walls are lined with carpets and fabric hangings. Furniture is usually pushed up against the walls, leaving most of a room empty.

People shop inside the huge Dordoi Bazaar in Bishkek.

that is increasing. Urban areas include not only the cities themselves but also the densely populated territories that usually surround them.

There are 32 official cities in Kyrgyzstan, with the largest, by far, being the capital, Bishkek, with a population of about 1,012,500. The city center is dominated by wide boulevards and stately, marble-faced public buildings. Ala-Too Square is the location of many state events and celebrations, as well as, on occasion, public demonstrations and protests. Compared with other capital cities around the world, Bishkek is not particularly cosmopolitan—there are relatively few foreigners—nor is it a very tourist-filled town.

Governmental and urban architecture is in the Soviet style, as that is when the buildings were constructed. Also, the nomadic Kyrgyz tradition produced no urban architectural style of its own. Cities were designed with many parks and plazas filled with benches that focused on monuments to Soviet achievements.

People live in large apartment blocks, where families live in two- or three-room apartments. Traditional-style bazaars sell a wide range of products, including food and handicrafts. On the outskirts of the city, there are also thousands of smaller, privately-built houses. Streets follow a grid pattern, with most flanked on both sides by narrow irrigation channels that water the trees shading the sidewalks.

Bishkek tends to be relaxed and easygoing. Office workers eat lunch in a park or an open-air café when the weather permits. For men, *chaykanas* (teahouses) are favorite gathering places. While women are permitted to enter, the chaykanas are considered special retreats for men. They are usually located in a tree-lined area near a stream. The men sit on a bed-size platform covered with a carpet and with a low table in the center. Fortified with endless cups of tea, the men can talk for hours.

Poor people live in crowded conditions on the edges of the city. Many scrounge out a living selling souvenirs, tobacco, and candy as street vendors.

The next largest town is Osh, located in the Fergana Valley, with a population of about 270,347. It's the oldest city in the country and is often referred to as the "capital of the south." Osh is located near the border of Uzbekistan and has a large percentage (about 58 percent) of Uzbek people. Its first Western-style supermarket opened in 2007, but most people still shop in the traditional markets.

RURAL LIFE

Roughly two-thirds of the nation's people live in rural areas, and for many, life has been hard since independence. Under Soviet rule, most rural families lived and worked on large collectives, herding or growing cotton and food crops. Now that herders and farmers are on their own, earning a living has proved more challenging, and many families live below the poverty line. Still, most eke out a living. Many are finding ways to add to their families' income. Some lead hunting parties, for example, and others guide hikers into mountainous

A little boy plays with soap bubbles near his family's yurts in Barskoon.

areas. With community-based tourism, some families make small sums by maintaining yurts for vacationers. In addition, a growing number of women are forming cooperatives to help them market their crafts, such as carpets and other felt objects.

Some people continue to live a semi-nomadic existence. For about 2,000 years, the remarkably mobile yurt formed the center of their lives. Most Kyrgyz today prefer the comfort of modern houses, especially in winter. When summer approaches, however, many miss the outdoor living and closeness to nature offered by a yurt. Some families move into yurts for the summer in high meadows, while others construct them in their gardens.

THE YURT: A SIGN OF THE NOMADIC PAST

For centuries the yurt—a portable circular dwelling of timber and felt or animal skin—has been a central part of the lives of Kyrgyzstan's nomadic peoples. Yurt *is the Turkish word for "home," and even though today's most common dwellings in Kyrgyzstan are brick structures or Soviet-style apartment blocks, the yurt still remains an iconic symbol of national identity. The yurt is represented on the flag by the design of the* tunduk, *the circular frame of wooden spokes around the smoke hole at the top. Yurts are now set up for festivals and funerals and are used in the summertime in gardens or when shepherds take their flocks high up in the mountains to graze.*

*The construction of a yurt has changed little over thousands of years. A framework of poplar poles (*kanats*) is bent and fixed with straps and leather nails into a domed circular tent. A trellis wall (*kerege*) is erected to keep the shape. Woven reed mats line the walls. Several thick layers of felt form the outside, and these are tied to strong poles dug into the ground. There is a smoke hole at the top, although today, people use stoves with chimneys. Inside, the yurts are often lined with brightly colored shyrdaks for warmth and comfort.*

The interior of a larger yurt is laid out in the traditional manner, with the left side reserved for men and their horses and hunting gear. The right side, for the women, contains the stove and cooking utensils. At the back, a richly carved cabinet or chest holds carpets and blankets for sleeping; these are spread out on the ground, which is covered with shyrdaks at night.

The portable yurt is easily assembled and carried from place to place on horseback or by wagon. In the past, the building of a new yurt was traditionally celebrated with great festivities. The words "May smoke always rise from this yurt! May the fire never go out in it" were spoken as a ram's head was tossed high into the air. The clan chief counted his subjects by the number of tyutyuns *(columns of smoke) rising from their yurts; this word is still used today in villages to tell how many households there are.*

The knowledge, skill, and tradition of yurt building is acknowledged by UNESCO as an element of Intangible Cultural Heritage of Humanity.

THE LIFE CYCLE

The Kyrgyz are fond of celebrations, and every major stage of a person's life is occasion for a feast. Not only is the birth of a child cause for a party, but there are also celebrations for a baby's naming, for the ninth day after birth, and even for the first haircut.

Marriage is one of the most important social functions because it strengthens the ties between families. Traditionally, marriages were arranged by the parents, and this practice is still followed in some rural areas. Usually the deal is struck when the boy is between 12 and 15 and the girl is a little younger. The ceremony is not held, however, until the two are grown. The celebrations typically involve feasts, fine clothing, and special sweets. Sons typically get married in order of their age, with the oldest going first. Thereafter, the oldest son's wife holds dominance over the other sons' wives in the family hierarchy.

The birth of a baby is a cause for great celebration in Kyrgyzstan.

GENDER ROLES

Under the Soviet system, women saw radically new opportunities open up for them in the areas of education and careers. In many ways, however, the old patriarchal (or male-dominated) system never disappeared. A woman, even when married, occupies the lowest status in the household, and normally she lives with her husband's family. She is not supposed to address the males in the family by name, referring instead to "your father's youngest brother." She usually wears a headscarf in the house and is expected to serve guests.

The most extreme illustration of the lingering male-dominated system is bride kidnapping. While the practice is now illegal and diminishing in Kyrgyzstan, there are several cases each year of a man running off with a woman he wants to marry. He takes her to his parents' home, then sends a message to her family requesting their permission. The family almost always agrees, since it

A woman wearing a traditional headscarf holds her small daughter in Arslanbob.

The Global Gender Gap Index for 2020 ranked the Kyrgyz Republic in 93rd place on a list of 153 countries. The index, created by the World Economic Forum, a not-for-profit foundation based in Geneva, Switzerland, tracks the discrepancies between men and women in four key areas: economics, education, health, and politics. The "gap" refers to the statistical distance between the two; the smaller the gap, the closer the genders are to parity, or equality, in a given society. For perspective, the number one country that year, with the smallest gap, was Iceland. The country with the greatest difference, at number 153, was Yemen. The United States ranked number 53.

Globally, women are finding more equality in the categories of health and education. In terms of economic opportunity and participation, they are significantly worse off, and in political empowerment, they are the furthest from achieving equality with men.

Likewise, Kyrgyzstan achieves near parity for women in health and educational attainment. It falls far short, however, in women's political and financial empowerment.

would bring shame on them to refuse. Usually, the kidnapped bride knows her abductor, and sometimes the couple plans it together as a romantic adventure. There are still instances, however, of actual bride kidnappings in which the man's identity is not known, and the woman's family tries everything in their power to get her back.

In spite of such traditions, most Kyrgyz women generally enjoy fewer restrictions on their lives than women in other Central Asian countries. They go to college, run businesses, and are also increasingly active in politics. In 2020, 19 percent of the seats in the Supreme Council were held by women.

FUNERALS

The Kyrgyz show a remarkable respect for the dead. A funeral is a large and expensive affair including an elaborate gravestone that is decorated with tiles and often features a dome or turret. The funeral ceremony lasts about 10 days, followed by a one-year period of mourning. Two yurts are constructed, one for female mourners, the other for the body of the deceased. The family of the deceased is expected to slaughter cattle and horses to serve visitors as they come to pay their respects.

Friends and family gather to mourn, with a great outpouring of emotion. Horse meat—the most expensive food—is served along with pilov, a rice-and-meat dish. After three days of mourning, the deceased is buried in a white cloth. In some tribes, a woman on a white horse reads a poem, then rides off. After that, women are excluded from the funeral.

For another seven days, men gather to read the Quran—the holy book of Islam. The Kyrgyz believe that the deceased is alone at that point and needs this companionship. Throughout the year of mourning, people visit the family and the cemetery. Finally, a year after the burial, the gravestone is erected. This is usually an occasion to slaughter an animal for a feast. Family members continue to visit the grave on holidays, such as Remembrance Day on June 13.

EDUCATION

Kyrgyzstan's education system suffered with the breakup of the Soviet Union. The nation's schools lost funding, and many of the nation's educators were

Shown here are Kyrgyzstani students and their teacher.

Shyrdaks are brightly colored, appliquéd felt carpets that can be seen across Kyrgyzstan. They are portable and light, and they have stylized portrayals of animals or plants sewn onto them. These bold felt carpets are still found in almost every home or yurt, just as they were thousands of years ago.

Shyrdaks are made by sewing together panels of felt, each with a stylized motif or image on it. Braid is then added to the outer edges. Traditionally, two colors were used, but the availability of artificial dyes since the 1960s has provided a broader array of bold, bright hues.

Groups of women typically work together to make the shyrdaks. The process involves several stages. First, the wool is cleaned by spreading it over wire mesh. Two women beat it for an entire day. Then, the layers of dyed or natural wool are spread on reed mats, and boiling water is poured over them. The mat is rolled up and tied with ropes, then trod or stomped on for two or three hours to fuse the wool into one layer. The mat is unrolled, and more boiling water is poured on it, after which it is rolled up a second time. The women then line up in a row and kneel on the roll, beating it with their arms for about half an hour. The mat is then unrolled, and the pressed wool is left to dry.

Patterns are drawn onto the wool with soap or chalk, and then cut out. These pieces are then stitched together, and a backing of felt is added. Both appliqués and background pieces are used, so nothing is wasted.

Russians, who promptly left for their homeland. Today, schooling is compulsory (mandatory) up to age 15. However, only 59 percent of boys and 56 percent of girls continue on into secondary school (grades 10—11). Even in the lower grades, absenteeism is high, with children in rural areas staying home to help the family with farming or herding. Children of nomadic migrants are particularly vulnerable to missing out on a consistent education, as are special needs children.

The quality of education is of particular concern. There is a serious lack of computers and other instructional technology in the schools; even textbooks are in short supply or are outdated. Teachers are underpaid and poorly trained. Although outside organizations such as UNICEF and the World Bank have established programs to boost educational quality in Kyrgyzstan, the problem continues to impede the country's progress. Adding to the challenge is that the government doesn't keep sufficient data on education across the nation. Without reliable statistics, international organizations—and even the Kyrgyzstani government itself—find it difficult to prescribe solutions.

DRESS STYLES

While Western-style dress is common today, particularly in the cities, traditional costumes remain important to Kyrgyzstanis. In their nomadic history, cold weather called for wearing many layers, often of furs and leathers.

In rural areas, women will wear long skirts and kerchiefs on their hair, like Russian babushkas. For special occasions, women wear long dresses with stand-up collars—or, instead of high collars, they might wear brightly colored vests and heavy jewelry. Under the *keynek* (long shirt or dress) women will wear loose leggings or pantaloons. Over the keynek, they wear an embroidered vest, and over that, a *chapan*, which is a long, padded robe or coat. In winter, men also wear chapans, often long sheepskin coats. A wide leather belt might cinch in the chapan and hold it in place.

Headgear is important to both men and women. At special events, women may wear fur-trimmed headdresses topped with crane feathers. An older woman often wears a turban—the number of times it is twisted and wound around her head indicates her status.

Men wear a white felt cap called an *ak-kalpak*. It is usually embroidered and has a tassel. In fact, the hat is so iconic that it's a national symbol and has a holiday devoted to it, March 5. In 2019, the cap was added to the list of UNESCO Intangible Cultural Heritage. The entry states: "More than eighty kinds of Ak-kalpak can be distinguished, decorated with various patterns bearing a sacred meaning and history. Environmentally friendly and comfortable, the Ak-kalpak resembles a snow peak, with four sides representing the four elements: air, water, fire and earth. The four edging lines symbolize life, with the tassels on the top symbolizing ancestors' posterity and memory, and the pattern symbolizing the family tree."

Kyrgyz nomads pose in traditional fancy clothes in front of a yurt in Issyk-Kul.

https://www.advantour.com/kyrgyzstan/traditions/kyrgyz-wedding.htm
This travel site discusses wedding traditions in Kyrgyzstan.

https://birdinflight.com/inspiration/project/20170713-elliott-verdier-kyrgyzstan.html
This photo essay reveals one man's glimpse into the lives of the Kyrgyzstanis.

https://ich.unesco.org/en/RL/ak-kalpak-craftsmanship-traditional-knowledge-and-skills-in-making-and-wearing-kyrgyz-mens-headwear-01496
https://ich.unesco.org/en/RL/traditional-knowledge-and-skills-in-making-kyrgyz-and-kazakh-yurts-turkic-nomadic-dwellings-00998
These are the UNESCO Intangible Cultural Heritage entries for ak-kalpak caps and yurts.

https://www.international.gc.ca/cil-cai/country_insights-apercus_pays/ci-ic_kg.aspx?lang=eng
This Canadian government site provides a good overview of Kyrgyz lifestyle, etiquette, and other characteristics of daily living in the country.

https://blog.nationalgeographic.org/2018/03/11/insight-into-kyrgyz-identity-through-hats-hijabs-and-other-types-of-head-coverings
This article discusses various kinds of Kyrgyzstani headgear and their importance.

https://triptokyrgyzstan.com/en/about-kyrgyzstan/customs-traditions/clothes
This travel site explains Kyrgyz traditional clothing.

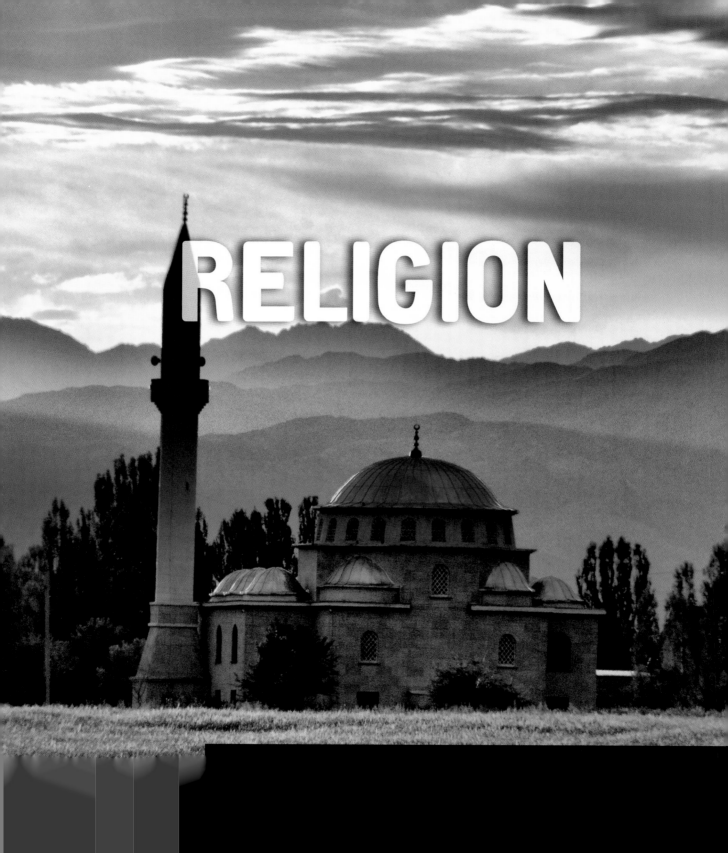

RELIGION

8

KYRGYZSTAN IS PRIMARILY AN Islamic nation. That is, most people identify themselves as Muslims. However, the country differs from many other Muslim-majority nations—particularly the Arab states, such as Saudi Arabia, Iraq, and 20 other countries in the Middle East and North Africa. Unlike most of those, Kyrgyzstan is fairly neutral when it comes to religion. Its constitution recognizes freedom of religion, and its government is secular.

The Kyrgyzstanis themselves, in general, are less conservative than many other Muslims. They consider themselves Sunni Muslims (the largest of two main denominations) but regard the religion as more of a cultural identity than a rigid doctrine. Like most Central Asians, their version of Islam is Hanafi, the oldest and most liberal of four Sunni schools of Islamic law. It is characterized by tolerance, flexibility, and reliance on reason. It values belief over practice. For example, many Kyrgyzstanis celebrate the Islamic holidays but don't follow daily Islamic practices.

A mosque is an Islamic house of worship, a gathering place for prayer. Typically, it includes a high tower called a minaret. Historically, a man called a *muezzin* would call the people to prayer five times a day from atop the minaret. Another characteristic of a mosque is the dome, which from the inside of the building represents the vault of heaven.

Kyrgyz Muslims pray on the first day of Eid al-Adha (Feast of the Sacrifice) at a mosque in Bishkek.

In recent years, this temperate attitude has been changing—particularly in the south of Kyrgyzstan—as groups from outside the country build mosques and encourage a stricter adherence to Islamic law.

HOW ISLAM CAME TO CENTRAL ASIA

Islam means "to submit" in Arabic. A Muslim submits to the will of God (Allah), which was revealed over many centuries through the prophets. They include many figures recognized by Judaism and Christianity, such as Abraham (Ibrahim), Moses (Musa), and Jesus (Isa). (Islam regards Jesus as a prophet but not as the son of God, which is how he is seen by Christians.) For Muslims, the last and greatest of those prophets was Muhammad, to whom the "Word of Allah" was revealed by the angel Gabriel. Those revelations make up the Quran (sometimes spelled Qur'an or Koran), the holy book of Islam. Muhammad therefore is not worshipped as God but is revered as a messenger of God.

THE FIVE PILLARS

Under the Five Pillars of Islam, devout Muslims are to:
1. *believe that "there is no other God than Allah, and Muhammad is his Prophet;"*
2. *obey the five daily calls to public prayer;*
3. *fast during daylight hours throughout the holy month of Ramadan;*
4. *pay a special tax to help the poor; and*
5. *if physically able, make at least one pilgrimage to the holy city of Mecca in Saudi Arabia.*

The prophet Muhammad founded the new religion in Medina, in what is now Saudi Arabia, in 622 CE. Although he died a mere 10 years later, his followers quickly established a vast empire. Spread mostly by Arab armies, the new religion caught on rapidly throughout the Mediterranean world, much of the Middle East, and then across Central Asia.

Initially, most of the nomadic tribes did not embrace the new religion. This was especially true in the region of present-day Kyrgyzstan, where Islam only became the official religion in the 10th century, and even then the conversion was piecemeal. As with so many elements of culture and cultural borrowing, the Kyrgyz adopted those Islamic beliefs and practices that met their needs and discarded the rest. For example, they never fully adopted the Five Pillars of Islam, even though these are regarded as the religion's basic principles. When a mullah (Islamic religious teacher or clergy) was available, he would conduct weddings, funerals, and daily prayers. If no mullah was in the village, the people proceeded on their own.

Early in the 19th century, when the khanate of Kokand gained control of the country, the khan's officials tried to oversee a more thorough conversion to Islam. This was quite successful in the southern part of Kyrgyzstan, close to the devout Muslims of Uzbekistan. North of the Tian Shan mountains, however, people were more heavily influenced by Russian industry and culture, so that region remained more secular. To this day, these differences in religious belief still contribute to the ongoing tensions between northern and southern Kyrgyzstan.

YEARS OF UPHEAVAL

Kyrgyzstan experienced years of painful and chaotic change in the 20th century. The Soviet takeover after 1917 involved a sweeping economic revolution, one that brought the Kyrgyz nomadic way of life to an abrupt end. The nomadic people were ordered to turn their herds and flocks over to the state and to move onto huge collective farms. Those who resisted were dealt with harshly; often they were banished to forced labor camps in Siberia or were executed.

Many people found that Islam offered some solace during these troubled times. They began attending prayer services in mosques and made pilgrimages to holy shrines. It was not long, however, before Soviet authorities cracked down on organized religion. Land and property owned by all religious groups—Christians, Jews, Buddhists, and Muslims—were confiscated. Religious leaders were persecuted.

From 1932 to 1936, Soviet leader Joseph Stalin supervised a campaign called "Movement of the Godless," his determined drive to create a religion-free state. Mosques were closed or destroyed. Mullahs were arrested as spies or enemy agents. Of the 47,000 mullahs who had served throughout Central Asia in 1930, only 2,000 were still alive by 1941.

The Kyrgyz response to the repression was to move their religious observances underground. A mystical sect called the Sufis helped to keep the practices intact. During World War II, in order to boost wartime morale, Stalin eased up on his brutal campaign. However, as soon as the war ended, the campaign resumed. In addition, the Soviets tried to promote atheism (having no belief in the existence of a god) as superior to any religion. During the 1950s, for example, the Tian Shan Komsomol (the youth branch of the Communist Party) sponsored hundreds of lectures on topics such as "What Every Atheist Should Know."

Then, during a period in the 1960s known as the "Khrushchev Thaw," Soviet premier Nikita Khrushchev changed direction. He decided that the traditional Kyrgyz way of life was better suited to the steppe environment than collective farms growing cotton. Suddenly, rural Kyrgyz were able to return to their beloved semi-nomadic life, moving their livestock to the high pastures for the summer months.

With independence, full freedom of worship was restored, and the government instituted an official policy of tolerance of all religions. There has been a flurry of mosque building throughout the country, although this is less noticeable in the north, where Islam is still not widely practiced.

RISE OF RADICAL ISLAM

The September 11, 2001, terrorist attacks in the United States, which were carried out by Islamic extremist (or Islamist) terrorists, sent shock waves across Central Asia. In addition to allowing the United States to establish an air base near Bishkek (it closed in 2014), the Kyrgyzstani government began monitoring the activities of Islamic organizations.

As radical Islamic fundamentalism and jihadist groups began rising in the early 21st century throughout the Middle East and North Africa, some Central Asians joined the movements. About 850 Kyrgyzstanis left their country to fight alongside these groups. Most Kyrgyz have no interest in Islamic fundamentalism, but radical groups often succeed in countries prone to political instability, and Kyrgyzstan is vulnerable.

In 2017, the Kyrgyz government approved a national program on countering extremism and terrorism for 2017 to 2022, with an action plan based on three priorities: (1) the prevention of extremism and terrorism, (2) the detection and suppression of extremism and terrorism, and (3) the improvement of legislative and other governmental means in combating extremism and terrorism. The plan focuses on empowering young people to recognize, understand, and resist radicalization.

OTHER RELIGIONS

About 7 percent of Kyrgyzstanis are Christians. The Russians brought the Russian Orthodox Church to the country in the late 19th century, and it remains a small presence there today. Prior to the Soviet era, Roman Catholic missionaries came to Kyrgyzstan by way of China but gained few adherents. Today, the Catholic Church mainly serves what's left of the German population

in the country. Seventh Day Adventists, Baptists, Jehovah's Witnesses, and others have also tried to gain converts.

The great majority of Kyrgyz have expressed little interest in changing their religion. They consider themselves to be Muslims, even if they have never entered a mosque and do not answer the daily calls to prayer. Especially during the uncertainty of recent years, Islam continues to be a unifying force, one that has provided stability for Kyrgyz culture.

Like other elements of Kyrgyz culture, the practice of Islam includes beliefs from nomadic days that have been fused with standard Islamic ideas and practices. A holy site often includes a wishing tree, for example, a carryover from a pre-Islamic belief system. Other ancient practices include consulting with non-Muslim holy men, or shamans.

An Orthodox Christian priest offers communion to a parishioner during a church service on Christmas Eve in Bishkek.

SUFISM

Sufism is a form of Islamic mysticism that began very early in the religion's history. Sufis are deeply religious or mystical people who seek a more direct union with God through deep prayer and other devotional practices. They follow a variety of "paths" to achieve a trancelike state that enables their spirits to unite with God.

In the early years of Islam, many Sufis acted as missionaries. They were particularly active along the Silk Road, where they easily adopted or incorporated the indigenous worldviews and spiritual beliefs of pre-Islamic Central Asia. Sufism flourished throughout the region. Another thing that made Sufism attractive to the Kyrgyz nomadic people was music. The nomadic Kyrgyz culture greatly valued music, songs, wisdom poetry, and epic narrations. Sufis, unlike conventional Muslims, made much use of music, so the two cultures easily interacted and intertwined.

SHAMANISM

Shamanism may well be the world's oldest belief system, dating to prehistoric times. It isn't an organized religion but consists of practices based on the idea that everything on earth and in the heavens contains a spirit. Through the efforts of a shaman, this spirit world can be contacted to help humans in some way, such as healing or revealing the future. A shaman is a practitioner who acts as an intermediary between the natural world and the world of the spirits, or supernatural world. A shaman may use magical rites to cure the sick or influence future events. The word for "shaman" in the Kyrgyz language is *bakshi*. Throughout history, both men and women have been shamans, and in Kyrgyzstan today, many shamans are women.

This shaman carries a traditional magic stick covered with carved symbols.

Carved stones called balbals can still be seen in fields and meadows in Kyrgyzstan.

Shamans were a basic part of tribal life during the centuries when the people of Central Asia were mostly nomadic. The people's strong dependence on the forces of nature naturally fostered animistic beliefs. (Animism is a belief that everything has a spirit.) Evidence of shamanism can be seen among the steppes and pastures, where stone figures, called *balbals*, are scattered. Near Bishkek, a group of balbals has been marked off as a sort of open-air museum. These date as far back as the sixth century. Balbals are thought to represent defeated opponents or deceased khans. Sometimes, graves were excavated from below these stone figures.

The shaman often gave advice about such matters as when to move the herds and flocks, when to go into battle, or when to retreat. Warriors often requested that a shaman make a ritual sacrifice on the eve of battle, so as to ensure a favorable outcome. Through a variety of different practices, the shaman entered a trance, enabling him or her to travel to different spirit worlds. These travels are described in Kyrgyzstan's eloquent epic poems and songs.

One of the major roles of shamanism has been in healing, and it is as healers that most shamans continue to function today. Rural Kyrgyz families are likely to seek a shaman for a medical problem while also going to a doctor. Some shamanistic practices can even be carried out without a shaman present, such as waving a smoking juniper branch around the house to ward off evil spirits.

The shamanist belief system predates Islam in Kyrgyzstan, and elements of it remain today or are being revived. In many cases, shamanism is mixed with Islam to create a syncretic (fusion) form of the religion.

INTERNET LINKS

https://central.asia-news.com/en_GB/articles/cnmi_ca/features/2018/07/16/feature-01
This article describes a law to increase government oversight of religion in Kyrgyzstan.

https://www.globalsecurity.org/military/world/centralasia/kyrgyz-religion.htm
This site looks at religion in Kyrgyzstan.

https://insideislam.wisc.edu/2011/03/the-bubu-shaman-women-of-kyrgyzstan
This article takes a quick look at Kyrgyzstan's Bubu shaman women.

https://thediplomat.com/2019/08/kyrgyzstan-attempts-to-isolate-local-islam
This article looks at the interaction of Islam and the Kyrgyzstani government.

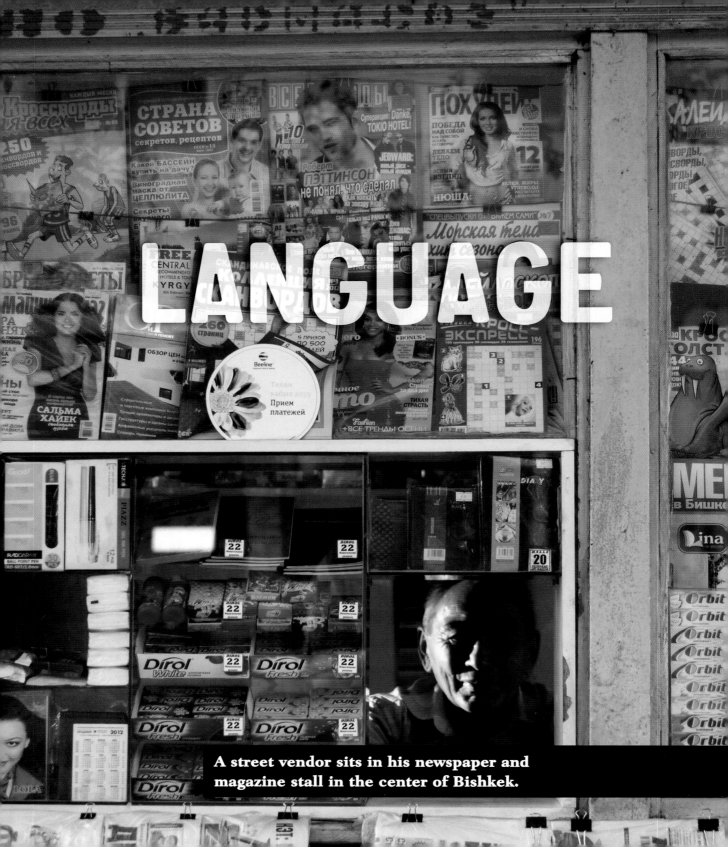

LANGUAGE

A street vendor sits in his newspaper and magazine stall in the center of Bishkek.

9

I T'S SAID THAT THE KYRGYZ PEOPLE love the sounds of their homeland's traditional poems and songs. They admire a well-spoken person, who speaks clearly and fluently. Given the profound role that a literary oral tradition has played in the Kyrgyz heritage, the auditory aspects of spoken language would naturally be highly valued.

Nevertheless, the more recent history of the Soviet era had a strong influence on how Kyrgyzstanis communicate today. For the generations who were forced to learn Russian first, it has been a struggle to reconnect with the language of their ancestors.

THE TWO-LANGUAGE SITUATION

Throughout the Soviet era, the dominant language spoken in Kyrgyzstan was Russian. Indeed, the Soviets insisted that all its republics adopt and teach Russian as the primary language as a way of unifying its far-flung regions. People quickly learned that it was the language of the educated and that speaking it fluently was essential for advancement in government. The Kyrgyz language was tolerated, but it became the social language—used at home and on the street.

Soon after independence was achieved in 1991, the government announced that Kyrgyz would be the new state language. However, the announcement sparked little change, and language usage remained much

It's difficult to transcribe a language into a different alphabet. There is as yet no commonly accepted system of writing the Kyrgyz language using the Latin, or Western, alphabet, which is a process called romanization. That's one reason Kyrgyz words and place names have so many different spellings in English texts. A system based on the Turkish alphabet is gaining popularity but is not yet universal.

as it had been before. Many Kyrgyz were startled to discover how spotty their knowledge of their own language was. At the same time, Russians and members of other minorities resisted having to learn the complicated Kyrgyz language.

The establishment of Kyrgyz as the state language increased the tensions between northern and southern Kyrgyzstan. Many young southern Kyrgyzstanis headed for Bishkek and other cities after independence, hoping to find work. They discovered that northern young people, often applying for the same jobs, tended to have an advantage because they spoke Russian and some Kyrgyz, while rural southerners spoke Kyrgyz only. Tensions ran so high that the conflict sometimes became violent.

Under pressure from ethnic Russians and other Russian speakers, the government adopted Russian as a second official language in 1997. Today, Russian remains the main language in the main cities, especially Bishkek, while Kyrgyz continues losing ground, especially among the younger generations. Nevertheless, Kyrgyz remains the most popularly spoken language in the country, particularly in rural areas.

MODERN KYRGYZ

Kyrgyz is spoken by about 4.1 million people in Kyrgyzstan and in certain regions of adjacent countries as well, including China, Afghanistan, Kazakhstan, Uzbekistan, and Tajikistan. Modern-day language convergence has trended toward an increasing degree of mutual intelligibility between the languages of Kyrgyz and Kazakh.

Kyrgyz is a Turkic language that has much in common with Turkish, Kazakh, Tartar, Azeri, and Uzbek. In fact, Uzbek is the second most commonly spoken language in the country, with Russian being third. (Russian, being a Slavic language, has almost nothing in common with Kyrgyz or the other Turkic languages.) Uzbek is widely spoken in the southern part of the country, where the majority of Kyrgyzstan's ethnic Uzbeks live. In fact, the Uzbek language has influenced the Kyrgyz spoken in this region such that it can be difficult for a Kyrgyz speaker from the north and a Kyrgyz speaker from the south to understand one another.

ALPHABETS

Although the ancient Kyrgyz language, much like Old Turkic, was originally written in Turkic runes, the modern written language emerged using the Perso-Arabic alphabet. Still, it didn't have a standard written form until 1923. In 1928, the Latin (Roman, or Western) script was instituted, but it didn't last long. In 1940, the Soviet dictator Joseph Stalin insisted on the exclusive use of the Cyrillic alphabet in all Soviet republics. The Russian language used the Cyrillic script, but it was insufficient for the sounds of the Kyrgyz language. Extra symbols had to be added, which proved cumbersome.

When Kyrgyzstan first became independent, there were plans to convert to the Latin (Western) alphabet, but it was never implemented. In neighboring

Different types of spices are displayed in bags at the Osh Bazaar in Bishkek. The names of the spices are written using Cyrillic letters, but prices are written in the same Arabic numerals that are used in the West.

Here are some English phrases and their Kyrgyz and Russian equivalents:

English	Kyrgyz	Russian
Hello.	Salam.	Privet
My name is	Menim atym	Menya zovut . . .
What's your name?	Sizdin atyngyz kim?	Kak tebya zovut?
Good-bye	Jakshy kalyngyz	Proshchay
How are you?	Kandaysyz?	Kak ty?
Yes/No	Ooba/Jok	Da/Nyet
Thank you	Rakhmat	Blagodaryu vas
bread	nan	khleb
meat.	et	myaso
rice	kuruch	ris
tea.	chay	chay

Kazakhstan, on the other hand, the government officially switched in 2018 to a Latin alphabet, similar to the one used in Turkey. (Azerbaijan and Turkmenistan, also former Soviet republics in Central Asia, switched away from the Cyrillic alphabet when they first became independent.) The Kazakh language is similar to Kyrgyz, as both are Turkic in origin.

On the other hand, Kyrgyzstan, like Russia, uses Arabic numerals, and all vehicle license plates have internationally accepted numbers on them.

NONVERBAL COMMUNICATION

The Kyrgyz have a variety of ways of greeting one another, and the procedures are followed in an almost ceremonial way. When two men who are friends greet each other, for example, the handshake is not overly vigorous, but it is warm and often quite elegant. Good friends can also shake hands by lightly and gently placing them, with the thumbs up, in between the other's hands. It is not unusual for men to simply touch wrists, especially when they are working and their hands might be dirty.

Women do not usually shake hands. Instead, each touches the other's shoulder, using the right hand. As a sign of respect, a younger woman will kiss an older woman on the cheek.

The Kyrgyz are also fond of hugging. Any festive gathering is likely to include lots of hugs.

INTERNET LINKS

https://www.omniglot.com/writing/kirghiz.htm
Omniglot offers an introduction to the Kyrgyz language and alphabet.

https://www.rferl.org/a/language_a_sensitive_issue_in_ kyrgyzstan/24246394.html
This article discusses the problems of multilingual Kyrgyzstan.

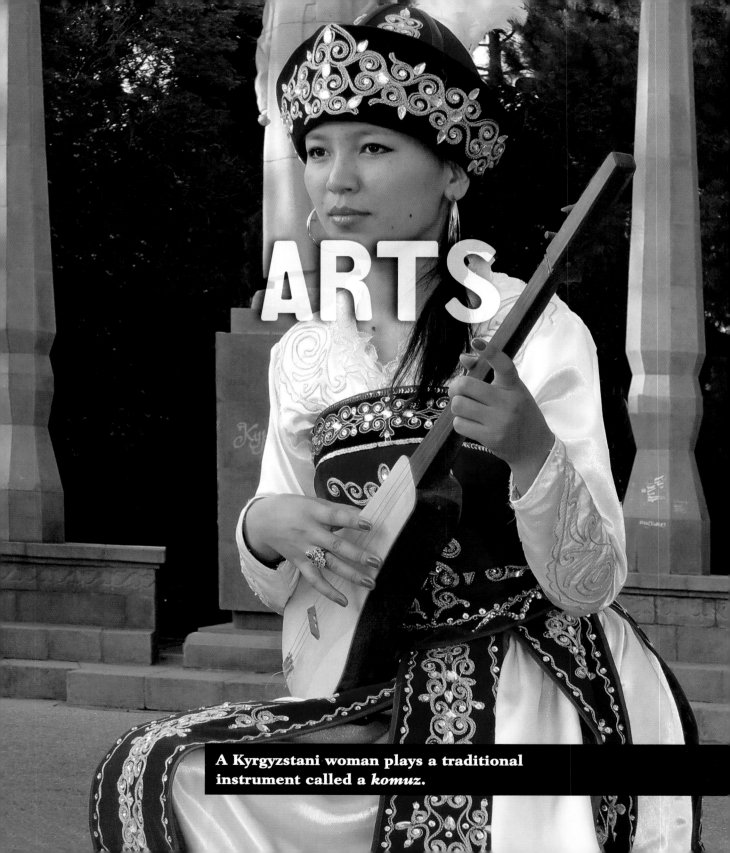

ARTS

A Kyrgyzstani woman plays a traditional instrument called a *komuz*.

10

T HE ARTS OF CENTRAL ASIA REFLECT
the long history of people who
followed a nomadic way of life.
Much of the region's art revolves
around horses, yurts, and the steppe
environment. The Kyrgyz made elaborately
carved yurt doors and beautifully
crafted saddles. Poems and songs were
inspired by simple natural events, such
as mist rising from a mountain lake
or an eagle soaring across a valley.

Kyrgyz art needed to be moved easily and quickly. The shyrdaks, or felt carpets, that decorated the walls of the yurt and added to its insulation were folded up in minutes, like the walls of the yurt itself. Beautifully crafted jewelry was not only an art form but also a convenient way to store and transport wealth. Storing tales, poems, and songs in one's memory was far easier than transporting a library of books.

AKYNS: TRAVELING BARDS

Kyrgyz literature is based on a long and remarkable oral tradition. For centuries, songs, stories, and poems were sung and recited by special

The National Musuem of Fine Arts in Bishkek contains 18,000 works of art: paintings, graphics, sculptures, and decorative artifacts. Fine art painting was never a native Kyrgyzstani art form, but during the Soviet era, some Kyrgyzstanis became artists. Some of their paintings are now exhibited in this museum. They depict a typical Soviet style, portraying the peasant or worker as noble and heroic.

Just as UNESCO (the United Nations Educational, Scientific and Cultural Organization) works to protect natural and cultural World Heritage Sites, it also identifies examples of "Intangible Cultural Heritage of Humanity" that need to be preserved. These include, according to the group's website, "traditions or living expressions inherited from our ancestors and passed on to our descendants, such as oral traditions, performing arts, social practices, rituals, arts, festive events, knowledge and practices concerning nature and the universe or the knowledge and skills to produce traditional crafts."

The Convention for the Safeguarding of the Intangible Cultural Heritage has listed nine elements for Kyrgyzstan. These include the traditional skills and knowledge in the making of men's headwear (ak-kalpak), flatbread, yurts, and traditional felt carpets (ala-kiyiz and shyrdak). They also include the art of akyns, Kyrgyz epic tellers; the epic trilogy of Manas, Semetey, and Seytek; the art of improvisation (Aitush); the traditional horse game (kok boru); and the celebration of Nowruz, the Islamic New Year.

performers called *akyns*. Each of these traveling minstrels, or bards, relied on a memorized repertoire of lyrics and tunes. When invited to a wedding, anniversary, or other celebration, the akyn recited long passages and improvised new lyrics to fit the special occasion.

In 2003, the "Art of Akyns, Kyrgyz Epic Tellers" was inscribed on the UNESCO list of Intangible Cultural Heritage of Humanity. The tradition began to wane in the 20th century, as Soviet life forced nomads to settle down and people learned to read and write. As a consequence, there are fewer practitioners nowadays, but in an effort to reconnect to their pre-Soviet identity, the Kyrgyz people are embracing beloved old traditions. Master akyns are training young apprentices, helped by state revitalization initiatives.

The Kyrgyz word *yr* refers to all the akyns' literary forms: poems, songs, and stories. All yrs carry a message—ethical, moral, or philosophical—designed to offer hope, encouragement, and sometimes guidance. They were particularly important in times of heavy warfare or during a conflict with another tribe.

The most honored of the akyns were called the *manaschi*. They were the narrators of a vast collection of oral stories called the Manas Epic.

THE MANAS EPIC

The Manas Epic is a cycle of oral legends and songs, some 20 times longer than the Greek classic The Odyssey. *Like the epics of other cultures, the Manas Epic tells of the origins of the Kyrgyz people—and how scattered tribes unified into one nation—through the many heroic deeds of a legendary warrior and his descendants. The cycle is split into three parts—"Manas; his son, "Semetey;" and his grandson, "Seytek."*

More than 1,000 years old (though some Western scholars dispute this), the collection of heroic tales consists of the myths, stories, and legends of the Kyrgyz people that have been passed on orally from generation to generation. Spoken continuously, it can take up to 13 hours to recite. It is such an integral part of the national identity that in 1995, the country celebrated the 1,000th anniversary of Manas. In 2013, UNESCO added the epic to its list of Intangible Cultural Heritage of Humanity, saying the trilogy "expressed the historical memory of the Kyrgyz people."

A statue of Manas stands in the Birinchi May district of Bishkek.

The hero of the epic may or may not have been a real, historical person, but it doesn't matter. Statues of Manas are found throughout Kyrgyzstan, and the country's main international airport is named for him. A sample of the verse describing the birth of Manas reflects his legendary aspects:

He is created from the beam between the Sky and the Earth,

He is created from the waves of a river under the moon,

He is created from the blend of gold and silver.

Manas embodies such virtues as bravery, justice, and national pride; he is always depicted as skilled in horsemanship and the martial arts. The oral tales and songs relate his adventures as he searches for a homeland for his people. As the tales unfold, they offer moral insight and guidance in how to deal with everyday problems.

The manaschi, *the special singers of the Manas Epic, are often trained in the profession from an early age. A child can receive a special calling when the Manas spirits come to him or her. Manaschi are traditionally men, although in recent years, women have also started to take on this role.*

MUSIC

All akyns have accompanied their recitation and improvisation with a variety of musical instruments. The most common of these is a three-stringed instrument called a *komuz,* or a *kyyak*, which is a similar instrument with two strings that is played with a bow. Other musicians might join in with wood, brass, horn, or clay instruments, producing haunting sounds. Percussion instruments are used to add important background sounds such as chimes and animal hooves pounding the hard earth. With or without accompaniment, skilled akyns can keep their audience enthralled for as long as 24 hours.

Traditional Kyrgyz folk songs are also popular in the nation, as are song-and-dance troupes. These groups play at urban nightclubs and also at community celebrations. The guitarlike komuz is the basic instrument, along with drums, flutes, long horns, and mouth harps (*temir komuz*) or a mouth harp that includes a string (*jygach ooz*).

WRITTEN LITERATURE

Kyrgyzstan does not have a strong tradition in conventional literary forms. Throughout most of the country's history, very few Kyrgyz could read and write. That changed when the Soviets set up a modern education system. Along with literacy, however, the Communists also brought an insistence on "socialist realism," the idea that the arts should depict the heroic struggle of workers and peasants against the oppressive capitalist system. The Kyrgyz had little interest in that kind of literary theme.

Chinghiz Aitmatov is shown here.

The one novelist who managed to rise above the limitations of the Soviet system was Chinghiz Aitmatov, the only Kyrgyz writer to achieve an international reputation. Beginning in 1963 with *Tales of the Mountains and Steppes*, Aitmatov produced a dozen highly praised novels. Writing first in Kyrgyz, then in Russian, he made keen observations about the country.

In the 1980s, Aitmatov dared to explore themes that had once been taboo under the Soviet regime. In *The Day Lasts Longer Than a Hundred Years* (1981) and *The Place of the Skull* (1989), he dealt with religious conflicts, environmental issues, and Kyrgyzstan's increasingly serious problem with illegal drugs.

HANDICRAFTS

Like other traditional Kyrgyz art forms, some handicrafts were lost in the 20th century as Russian arts were promoted and taught in their place. Kyrgyz embroidery, for instance, was replaced by Russian and Ukrainian styles and techniques.

Local artisans work together making a large *ala kiyiz* style of woolen carpet in Issyk-Kul.

One of the most iconic of Kyrgyz folk arts is the making of felt carpets, or shyrdaks—another art recognized by UNESCO as an example of Intangible Cultural Heritage. The practice dates back many centuries; the nomadic peoples learned to make felt as they acquired herds of sheep. Felt is a fabric produced by soaking wool in boiling water and applying a great deal of pressure, which makes the fibers stick together, no weaving necessary. It takes the wool from approximately five sheep to make one shyrdak rug. The process is slow and labor-intensive, and it is a task traditionally performed by women. The designs are based on colorful abstract shapes.

In recent times, the skill and craft were nearly lost—the domain of old, rural women. The younger generation showed little interest in learning it, and the easy availability of inexpensive synthetic carpets and the poor quality and low availability of the necessary raw materials only made it worse. The shyrdaks produced for tourists lacked the integrity of the older ones.

Today, however, some artisans are returning to more traditional designs and techniques. The artificial dyes of the 1960s produced brightly colored appliqués, for example, but many women are now going back to the softer tones created by natural dyes, such as those made from raspberry leaves, birch roots, and pear leaves. Neutral colors, without dyes, are also gaining popularity.

In addition to the shyrdaks, other handicrafts also reflect the nomadic past, when mobility was so important. *Ayak kaps*, for instance, are woven bags that are hung on yurt walls for storing plates, clothing, and other items. Embossed leather bottles are also still being made, and these were used for storing and transporting kymyz.

Kyrgyz craftspeople continue to produce outstanding jewelry, usually working with silver and semiprecious stones. In nomadic days, men carried their wealth in the form of swords and daggers that had jeweled handles and sheaths. Women's jewelry was equally elaborate and valuable. It was said that, when on the move, a wealthy woman might be wearing so much jewelry that walking was difficult. All of these items are sold today in city bazaars—and even online—some as antiques, others as replicas.

INTERNET LINKS

https://folkcloud.com/folk-music-by-country/kyrgyzstan
This folk music site has a page for Kyrgyz music with audio files.

https://ich.unesco.org/en/state/kyrgyzstan-KG
The Intangible Heritage elements for Kyrgyzstan are linked from this page.

http://www.silkroadfoundation.org/folklore/manas/manasintro.html
Portions of the Manas Epic are translated and explained on this site.

LEISURE

People enjoy sledding on inflatable toboggans
down snowy hillsides in Kyrgyzstan.

I N BISHKEK, LEISURE ACTIVITIES ARE much as they are in other modern cities. There are movie theaters, museums, restaurants, and city parks for relaxation or entertainment. For people without much money, however, leisure activities are few.

Outside the cities, the pace of life in Kyrgyzstan can be slow. In villages, subsistence living keeps people busy just getting by. In rural areas, life closely follows the seasons and the movement of the herds to and from the high summer pastures, or jailoos. People work hard, especially in the struggling post-Soviet economy, and they do not have much time for leisure. For women, especially, there is little to do outside the chores of housekeeping and child raising. However, women do get together to produce handicrafts, both as an income-producing activity as well as for social interaction and leisure.

Since the Kyrgyz have traditionally had a strong bond with the natural world, especially as nomadic herders, it is not surprising that they often spend their leisure time engaging in outdoor activities. There are few of the indoor activities familiar to Westerners. Television and movie theaters are found only in major urban areas, for example, and activities such as board games are uncommon, except for the ancient board game of *nard*, or backgammon. The Kyrgyz are not usually avid readers of books. However, many enjoy spending hours listening to the clever improvisation and recitations of the akyns.

Kyrgyzstan has little history in most of the Olympic sports, and despite its abundance of snowy mountains, it does not have a tradition of skiing. (Ice hockey, however, is gaining popularity.) Since independence, Kyrgyzstan has sent athletes to six Summer Games and five Winter Games and has won four medals, in judo and wrestling.

TEA DRINKING

Kyrgyz are fond of visiting family and friends, and this frequently involves the ceremony of drinking tea. The activity might take place in a home, in a yurt, or—in urban areas—in a chaykana, or teahouse.

People drink tea from a small bowl, a *piala*. The host often pours the first cup, then throws it away in order to clean the piala. Next, a piala of tea is poured out twice and returned twice to the pot to brew the tea. The piala for a guest is filled only partway, allowing the host to refill it often to keep it warm. Throughout this time-honored procedure, people talk. The combination of tea and conversation is considered a perfect way to spend an afternoon or evening.

BAZAARS

Every town has a colorful market, or bazaar, and a favorite pastime, especially on Sundays, is to spend the day there. Some are essentially farmers' markets. The stalls are piled high with fresh and dried fruits, peanuts, walnuts, bread, eggs, meat, and honey.

A woman serves tea in a yurt in Song Kul.

Every bazaar also has a number of food stalls, each with its own specialty. The food is served with tea or *ayran*, a salty yogurt drink. In the continuing tough economic times, older women called *babushki*, or grandmothers, spread blankets outside the bazaar on which they arrange their items to sell: matches, pens and pencils, candies, and chewing gum.

One of the most popular bazaars is the *mal bazari*, or animal market, on the northern edge of Karakol. Hundreds of people gather for the Sunday event, some having traveled for several days. They represent the wide diversity of

Central Asian ethnic groups, and they come to buy and sell horses, cattle, sheep, goats, pigs, and sometimes a camel. It is a noisy, festive scene marked at times by the excitement of someone test-riding a horse by galloping through the crowd.

In Karakol, people come to the weekly outdoor animal market, one of the largest markets of this sort in Central Asia.

HUNTING, FISHING, AND GUIDING

For many Kyrgyz, activities such as hunting and fishing are often means of providing a little extra food or income for the family. A short trip by vehicle or on horseback in any direction can lead to the spectacular scenery and hunting grounds that Kyrgyzstan is famous for. A small number of Kyrgyz still employ one unique way of hunting—by using a golden eagle. In nomadic days, hunting with eagles was quite common, and there are still a few hundred practitioners

A man holds a golden eagle trained in the traditional Kyrgyz hunting arts of the Eurasian steppes.

today. A trained eagle can bring down small game such as rabbits or foxes. Spectators enjoy the speed and skill that are displayed. Hunters sometimes use falcons too.

The lakes and streams of Kyrgyzstan are teeming with fish. A typical fisherman on a stream feeding Lake Issyk-Kul might expect to catch four or five trout every hour. Foreign visitors as well as Kyrgyzstanis visit the country's pristine lakes, such as the seven famous lakes at the Sary-Chelek Biosphere Reserve.

As the number of foreign visitors has increased, more and more Kyrgyz are earning money by acting as tour guides. Visitors from Europe and the United States come for trekking, mountaineering, and rock climbing. These visitors have discovered that Kyrgyzstan has some of the world's most spectacular scenery and that local guides are essential to make the most of the experience.

The Kyrgyz, in turn, have the opportunity to enjoy these leisure activities while they earn some money.

The nation's beautiful, unspoiled mountains and valleys have proved increasingly popular. A trek can be a hike of a few hours or an adventure ranging from a few days to three or four weeks, traveling either on foot, on horseback, or in a four-wheel-drive vehicle. Mountaineering is more rigorous and involves climbing peaks or struggling through rugged mountain passes.

SPORTS ON HORSEBACK

The Kyrgyz generally show little interest in sports that are popular in the West, such as soccer, golf, or sailing and boating. However, no other society in the world is more famous for its equestrian games. These sporting contests, some dating back 1,000 years or more, are fast-paced, rough, and sometimes violent. While the games are not as common as in the nomadic past, almost any modern festival is an opportunity for these wild and colorful sports.

At Lake Issyk-Kul, a woman competes in the specialized sport of archery on horseback.

The best-known of the equestrian sports is called *kok boru*. Kok boru is recognized as an element of UNESCO's Intangible Cultural Heritage, which reports, "The element is an expression of the cultural and historic tradition and spiritual identity of its practitioners and serves to unite communities regardless of social status, fostering a culture of teamwork, responsibility and respect."

The game is played with a headless goat, one that has also had its lower legs and entrails removed. After being soaked in cold water overnight to toughen it up, the goat carcass is placed in a circle at one end of a large field. At the other end of the field, any number of players wait, seated on their tough, wiry Kyrgyz horses. At the starter's signal, the players race across the field, competing either as individuals or as teams. One player grabs the carcass and tries to carry it down the length of the field, around a post, then back to the circle where he drops it and is declared the winner. Of course, a crowd of other riders is just as eager to stop him and take away the prize.

To spectators, the game appears to be a chaotic war on horseback. Men and horses come together in a wild, noisy struggle, until one rider will suddenly

Teams from Russia and Kazakhstan play the traditional sport of kok boru, also known as buzkashi, during the World Nomad Games 2018 in Cholpon-Ata, in eastern Kyrgyzstan.

break loose, dragging the carcass with the others in pursuit. According to legend, the game originated as a military training exercise in the days of Genghis Khan to develop the kind of daring and skill that warriors needed.

Other equestrian games are also popular, both for participants and for spectators. These games are usually played in the cooler months of spring and autumn. In a game called *tyin enmei*, participants try to pick coins off the ground while riding at full gallop. *Jumby atmai* is archery on horseback, and in *oodarysh*, contestants wrestle while on horseback. A *chabysh* is a more traditional horse race, but it is run over a distance of 15 to 20 miles (24 to 32 km). All of these games involve prizes, such as money, a rifle, or a *chapan* or cloak.

In a game called *kyz kuumai* ("chasing after the bride"), a man chases a woman, both on horseback, and tries to catch her and kiss her. The woman is given a head start as well as the faster horse. If the woman successfully avoids her pursuer, she gets to chase the humiliated man and, when she catches him, give him a few whacks with her whip.

INTERNET LINKS

https://ich.unesco.org/en/RL/kok-boru-traditional-horse-game-01294
The Intangible Heritage listing for kok boru is on this page.

FESTIVALS

Crowds gather for Independence Day
celebrations on August 31 in Bishkek.

12

THE KYRGYZ RARELY PASS UP AN opportunity for a celebration. The occasion might be a family event, such as a wedding or the birth of a child, or it might be a formal festival celebrating a day of national importance, such as Independence Day.

The festivals are celebrated according to ancient tradition, dating back hundreds of years. Whenever a khan was newly elected, a great festival was held that brought together tribal leaders from across Central Asia. The great festivals included then, as they do today, an enormous feast, games on horseback, and storytelling and songs by the akyns, weaving in any new tales about recent events or new leaders.

PATRIOTIC HOLIDAYS

Like most countries, Kyrgyzstan commemorates important historical events. These are observed with flags, parades, and political speeches. Independence Day, on August 31, is the major state holiday. It marks the day Kyrgyzstan became an independent nation, free of Soviet control. The long decades of Soviet rule left a cultural mark on the new nation, however, and Kyrgyzstan still observes some special occasions from those times.

One is Defender of the Fatherland Day in February. Also called Defense of the Motherland Day, it's a time to honor people who have served in the military. Another, Victory Day on May 9, commemorates the triumph of the Soviet Union over Nazi Germany at the end of World War II. Yet another Soviet leftover, the Day of the Great October Socialist Revolution,

In 2014, 2016, and 2018, the World Nomad Games were held in Cholpon-Ata, Kyrgyzstan. The event, created in 2014, celebrates the sports of the nomadic peoples of Central Asia—such as horse racing, falconry, kok boru, archery, wrestling, and mancala games. Athletes compete from all the Central Asian countries, as well as from Mongolia, Russia, and Turkey. In 2020, the games were held in Turkey.

which commemorated the Russian Revolution of 1916, was renamed in 2017 in Kyrgyzstan. Now celebrated as the Days of History and Memory of Ancestors, the November holiday has a new purpose as well.

May 5 is Constitution Day in Kyrgyzstan; it marks the adoption of the country's first post-Soviet constitution in 1993. An even newer patriotic observance, introduced in 2016, is the Day of the People's April Revolution. It marks the day in 2010 that protesters stormed the parliament building in Bishkek, which led to the ouster and resignation of President Kurmanbek Bakiyev.

RELIGIOUS HOLIDAYS

Being a predominantly Muslim country, Kyrgyzstan observes the Islamic holy days. These follow the dates of the lunar Islamic calendar, which is different from the Western calendar. Therefore, those special occasions revolve through

Kyrgyzstani men and boys pray together during Eid al-Adha in Bishkek's central square.

the seasons and fall on different days each year. Kyrgyzstan, like other Muslim nations, uses the Western calendar for nonreligious dates so as to be in sync with the rest of the world. It also observes the Western New Year's holiday January 1.

The two most important Muslim festivals are the *eids*—Eid al-Fitr and Eid al-Adha. In Kyrgyzstan they are called Orozo Ait and Kurman Ait. Of the two, the most solemn is Kurman Ait (Eid al-Adha), the Feast of the Sacrifice. It commemorates the sacrifice of Abraham, who offered his son as a sacrifice because he believed that it was God's wish. God was pleased with Abraham's obedience and spared his son. This story is from the Old Testament, a biblical text sanctified by Muslims as much as by Jews and Christians.

Orozo Ait, or Eid al-Fitr, is a celebration at the end of the month of Ramadan. Ramadan, the ninth month of the Islamic year, is a holy time of directing thoughts to God and fasting during the daylight hours. From sunrise to sunset, observant Muslims do not eat or drink, not even water. When the month ends, great feasting and joy characterize the celebration of Eid-al-Fitr. While some Muslims in Kyrgyzstan are devout, many others are only moderately observant and may not fast through the entire month, or even at all. Nevertheless, they are happy to enjoy the time of Orozo Ait. In addition to the feasting, it's a time to visit friends and family, give little gifts to children, and give food and charity to the needy.

NOWRUZ

Nowruz, or Nooruz, (New Day) is one of the most popular festivals in all of Central Asia, also observed by many Afghans and Iranians as well as Kurds in Iraq, Turkey, and Syria. This special day features a unique array of foods. It began more than 1,000 years ago as a shamanistic celebration of the arrival of spring. Over time, the festival became wrapped in the practices of Islam. It takes place on March 21, the spring equinox.

In the mid-20th century, Soviet authorities banned the festival, fearing that it might weaken people's loyalty to the Soviet system. In 1989, as the Soviets were loosening restrictions, they reversed their position. Nowruz again became an official holiday, but as a secular event, with no religious overtones.

A Kyrgyz family picnics during the celebrations of Nowruz in Bishkek on March 21, 2019.

Today, it is celebrated with great fanfare, including street fairs, storytelling, games on horseback, and feasting. Some of the dishes that are prepared are unique to this holiday. One traditional dish, prepared only by women, is *sumalak*. It is made with wheat that has been soaked in water for three days until it sprouts. The wheat is then ground; mixed with oil, flour, and sugar; and then cooked over low heat for 24 hours.

Another dish is *halim*, a mixture of boiled meat and wheat grains, seasoned with black pepper and cinnamon. Still another dish is *nishalda*, made from whipped egg whites, sugar, and licorice flavoring. The Nowruz table always includes seven items, all beginning with the sh sound: *sharob* (wine), *shakar* (sugar), *shir* (milk), *shirinliklar* (candy or dessert), *sharbat* (sherbet), *sham* (a candle), and *shona* (a flower bud, symbolizing the renewal of life).

January 1. . . . . . *New Year's Day*
January 7. . . . . . *Russian Orthodox Christmas*
February 23 . . . . *Defender of the Fatherland Day (Men's Day)*
March 8 . . . . . . *International Women's Day*
March 21 . . . . . . *Nowruz (Spring Festival)*
April 7 . . . . *People's April Revolution Day*
May 1. . . . . *May Day (Labor Day)*
May 5. . . . . *Constitution Day*
May 9. . . . . *Victory Day*
August 31 . . . . . *Independence Day*
November 7–9 . . . *Days of History and Memory of Ancestors*
Variable dates . . . *Orozo Ait (Eid al-Fitr)*
. . . . *Kurman Ait (Eid al-Adha)*

In addition to feasting, music, dance, and the traditional equestrian games, people join hands around a burning juniper log in the hope of having a good harvest.

FAMILY CELEBRATIONS

Family celebrations, or those involving just the local community, generally follow the same pattern as the great national festivals. The building of a new yurt, for example, includes the usual feast, the telling of witty stories, dancing, and then special rituals. A typical ceremony involves tossing the head of a ram into the air while shouting the words: "May smoke always rise from this yurt! May the fire never go out in it!" In the past, even breaking camp when the tribe moved on involved a special custom. Everything was done according to a set pattern, accompanied by special songs.

Other celebrations vary, depending on the occasion. Certain rituals and foods are associated with different events in a child's life. Jentek Toi, for example, is a family festival celebrating the birth of a child; Kyrkan Chygaruu celebrates the 40th day after the birth; and Tushoo-Kyrkuu is the party for the first birthday. Another group of celebrations is for a wedding, including the announcement of the nuptials, the actual event itself, and the bride's first visit to her parents' home after the wedding.

Special meals are prepared for national festivals and for local celebrations. A bright white tablecloth is placed on a low, round table. The meal starts with a prayer and tea. Different kinds of bread are placed on the table, along with fruits and sweets. A variety of appetizers is served, along with kymyz, the country's favorite beverage, which is made from fermented mare's milk. One appetizer, for example, is *choochook*—a sausage made of specially prepared horse fat.

The main part of the meal is likely to include *beshbarmak*, a dish made of horse-meat sausage, broad noodles, and a sauce. Another favorite is *samsa*, a pastry filled with meat, onions, and the fat of a lamb's tail. (Kyrgyz sheep are a breed known for their large, fatty tails.) Samsa is cooked in a special clay oven

In Balasagun, Kyrgyzstan, people in Western attire dance at a wedding party.

called a tandor and is served straight from it. The meal is also accompanied by more kymyz or ayran, a salty, yogurt-based drink. More tea or, on special occasions, an alcoholic beverage called vodka conclude the meal.

OTHER SPECIAL FESTIVALS

During the summertime, special competitions and festivals are held in pastures throughout the country. To the consternation of some travel agencies, these festivals tend to pop up without much publicity and without set schedules or dates, making them difficult to promote to tourists. However, the local people generally know what's going on.

Among the most popular are the Horse Games Festivals and the Birds of Prey Festival. These involve traditional contests held in a carnival atmosphere. Often, traditional handicrafts, music, storytelling, wrestling, and foods are part of the fun.

In Bishkek and the Issyk-Kul Lake region, festivals of a more international flavor take place, including jazz, rock, and other arts and cultural events.

INTERNET LINKS

https://kyrgyzstan-tourism.com/events
This site lists special events throughout the country, some aimed mainly at tourists.

https://www.timeanddate.com/holidays/kyrgyzstan
This calendar site provides a list of public holidays and observances in Kyrgyzstan.

http://worldnomadgames.com/en
The official site for the World Nomad Games has articles, photos, and videos.

FOOD

Flatbreads cooked in a tandoori oven are displayed at the Osh Market in Bishkek.

13

THE HISTORY OF CENTRAL ASIA IS written in the cuisine of Kyrgyzstan. In some ways, it makes more sense to discuss Central Asian cuisine in general because the differences from one country to another are small. Kyrgyz cuisine is particularly similar to that of the Kazakhs (in Kazakhstan).

The nomadic lifestyle of former days can still be tasted in dishes heavy on meats—mutton (lamb), beef, and horse. Dairy products made from those same animals round out the traditional diet, along with bread, noodles, and rice. Nomadic people didn't stay in one place long enough to grow vegetables. They also didn't carry many spices or herbs with them, so traditional dishes tend to be rather plain. Breads that didn't require a long rise time and that cooked quickly were best for that lifestyle, and flatbreads were the perfect answer.

Most Central Asian nomads settled down over the course of the 20th century, mainly because they were forced to do so under Soviet rule. As people adopted a settled lifestyle, they developed, or borrowed, dishes such as pilafs, kebabs, noodles, and stews, plus fancy breads and pastries.

Today's diets, therefore, include elements of neighboring lands—particularly Russia—and other ethnic groups. The Uyghur (WEE-GUR) people, an ethnic group from northwestern China, contributed the popular noodle dish *laghman*. Uzbeks brought *plov*, a rice pilaf type of dish called *paloo* in Kyrgyzstan. Blini, thin rolled pancakes served with sour cream, cottage cheese, and jam, are a Russian favorite.

UNESCO considers the making and sharing of flatbread in Kyrgyzstan and several other countries (Azerbaijan, Iran, Kazakhstan, and Turkey) to be an example of Intangible Cultural Heritage. The communal practice of breadmaking and sharing expresses hospitality and solidarity, and it symbolizes common cultural roots.

Women in a shepherding family cook outside their yurt in the Suusamyr Valley of Kyrgyzstan.

POPULAR DISHES

Lamb is the most common meat in Kyrgyz cooking. The fat-tailed Kyrgyz sheep are prized for their meat as well as their wool. Fat from the sheep's tail is esteemed more highly than the meat itself. One of the most common ways to serve it is *shashlik* (lamb kebabs). Kebabs are also made of beef, chicken, or other chopped meats.

The dish that is commonly called the national dish of Kyrgyzstan is beshbarmak, a meal of boiled meat and noodles. Traditionally, horsemeat or mutton (lamb) is used. The dish was first prepared by Kazakh nomads. The name means "five fingers," which refers to eating it by hand. The broth served on the side is called *shorpa* (or *sorpa*). The whole dish can also be served as the soup, also by that name.

Pilov, plov, or paloo, is so commonplace that some travelers have assumed it was the only thing the Kyrgyz could cook. Pilov consists of rice with boiled or fried meat, onions, carrots, and raisins or fruit slices. This is a common dish served to guests.

Central Asian noodles, or laghman, are different from noodles found elsewhere. Laghman is often used as the base for a spicy soup—also called laghman—that includes fried lamb, peppers, tomatoes, and onions.

Two other popular soups are shorpa, made with boiled lamb and sometimes tomatoes, carrots, and turnips, and *manpar*, which consists of noodle bits, meat, and vegetables in a broth with mild seasoning. Salads are not a common, everyday food. In response to the requests of travelers, though, a *salat tourist* is served, consisting of sliced tomatoes and cucumbers. Other salad items, such as parsley, fresh coriander, green onions, and dill, are served and eaten separately.

Traditional seasonings are usually mild, but the sauces of other ethnic dishes can be extremely spicy. The most common spices are black cumin, red and black pepper, barberries, coriander, and sesame seeds. Common herbs include dill, parsley, celeriac (celery root), and basil. Wine vinegar and fermented milk products are also standard.

BREADS

Bread is considered so essential to the Kyrgyz diet that it's almost sacred. There are several forms, none of which resemble American sliced bread.

Nan, the flatbread that is served at every meal, is baked in tandoori ovens. This simple staple is sold in most places, and a traditional home meal is never complete without it. Some varieties are prepared with onions, meat, sesame seeds, or the fat from the tail of a sheep. *Lepyoshka*, which is Uzbek-style bread, is a thicker, circular loaf with a full, round crust. Something like a large, sauceless, no-cheese pizza crust, it's often imprinted with designs and sometimes sprinkled with seeds. This bread is seen across Kyrgyzstan and Central Asia.

Borsok (or *boorsok*) is a fried, puffed bread, made in small squares. It's often dunked into savory or sweet sauces or dips, such as honey or jam. *Katama* (or *kattama*) is another kind of fried bread, often made with onions.

Filled breads and dumplings are also popular. *Oromo* is a pie made of a noodle-like dough rolled around a filling of pumpkin and perhaps minced lamb or cabbage, and spiraled into a baking pan. *Samsy* are stuffed buns filled with minced meat and a fruit or vegetable, often horsemeat and pumpkin.

SNACKS

Various meat-and-dough snacks are sold by street vendors. Some are steamed meat dumplings; other varieties are boiled, baked, or fried. These can be served plain or with sour cream, butter, or vinegar. Another common street food is *piroshki*, a Russian fried pie stuffed with meat or potatoes.

Fruits are also popular. They are eaten fresh, cooked, dried, or made into jams, preserves, and a drink called *sokh*. Fruit in any form is the most common kind of sweet or dessert. Other favorite snack items include all kinds of nuts and dried fruits, including walnuts, peanuts, and almonds mixed with raisins and dried apricots.

DAIRY PRODUCTS

The Kyrgyz are fond of slightly fermented dairy products, especially kymyz (sometimes spelled *kumis*, *koumiss*, or other similar variations), which is mare's milk. The milk of cows, sheep, goats, and camels is also used. Soured milk is used to make yogurt. The yogurt can be strained to make *suzma*, a tart cream cheese used as garnish or added to soups. Another milk product is *kurtob*, which is dried suzma, shaped into small, marble-size balls. Kyrgyz carry these when they travel, since it is a nutritious snack that never spoils.

A nomadic woman stirs the horse milk to make kymyz.

BEVERAGES

Kymyz is the best-known Kyrgyz drink, but a runny yogurt called ayran is also popular, as is *maksym*, a thick drink made from wheat that is sold at street stalls during the summer. Tea is a more common mealtime drink.

Except for kymyz, alcoholic drinks were virtually unknown until the Russians arrived. Russian vodka, which the Kyrgyz call *arak*, has had an unfortunate impact on Kyrgyz society. Especially during hard economic times, drunkenness and alcoholism have become problems. German-made beers and a yeasty Russian drink called *kvas* are also available in restaurants.

DINING CUSTOMS

No matter how poor a Kyrgyz family is, the main meal follows common practices. In Muslim families, for example, the left hand is considered unclean,

A family sits on mats during lunch in Arslanbob.

so it is not used for handling food at the table. People receive dishes with their right hands and use only their right hands for raising food to their mouths.

A *dastarkhan* is a large cloth spread on the floor that serves as a dining table. People seated around a dastarkhan are careful not to step on it. When seated around the cloth, it is also customary not to let your foot point at any other diner.

Bread is regarded as a sacred food. Everyone at a meal is careful not to throw it away or place it on the ground. Whenever bread is offered, it is polite to break off a piece and eat it.

The *amin* is a prayer of thanks that ends the meal. No one eats after the amin. The prayer often consists of moving cupped hands over the face as if washing. Women as well as men commonly use this gesture.

HOSPITALITY

In Islamic cultures, a guest holds a position of honor, whether the person is Muslim or not. Hosts will extend every act of hospitality to a guest, even if they have very little food for themselves.

Upon entering the house, a guest will remove his or her shoes, and a pair of slippers or flip-flops will be provided. The host will offer water for washing the hands. After a prayer, tea, bread, and appetizers, the main dish is likely to be beshbarmak. Since the name means "five fingers," it is traditionally eaten with the hand (the right one, of course). However, large spoons may be used. Other festive dishes, including pilov, are also included, and bread is always present.

If the dinner is a special occasion, the host might have slaughtered a sheep for the meal. The parts of the sheep are divided in customary ways. The guest receives one of the choicest cuts, usually an eyeball, the brain, or meat from the right cheek. It would be a grave insult to refuse such an act of generosity. The meal usually ends with tea and a prayer.

INTERNET LINKS

http://factsanddetails.com/central-asia/Kyrgyzstan/sub8_5b/entry-4765.html
This entry offers an overview of Kyrgyzstan's cuisine, food culture, and dining customs.

https://silkroadexplore.com/blog/the-food-of-kyrgyzstan
This travel site gives a quick overview of Kyrgyzstani cuisine, with links to other articles.

BESHBARMAK

The Kyrgyz cook will typically make homemade noodles for this dish. For ease of preparation, however, this recipe substitutes fresh lasagna noodles or thick fresh egg noodles.

2 ½ pounds (1.2 kilograms) lamb or beef on
  the bone
1—2 large onions, peeled and cut into thick rings
1—2 bay leaves
salt, pepper
1 pound (0.5 kg) fresh noodles (if using lasagna
noodles, cut into thick strips)
finely sliced chives or chopped fresh dill,
  for garnish

Place the meat in a deep pot. Cover with cold water, bay leaves, and half of the onion rings. Add salt if desired. Bring to a boil, removing the fat or grease from the surface as needed.

Reduce the heat, cover the pot, and simmer for 2 and a half hours, or until the meat is soft and easily falls off the bone. Five minutes before the meat is done, add the remaining onion rings together with more salt and pepper. Using a slotted spoon, remove the meat and onions from the broth, and set aside. When cool enough to handle, remove the meat from the bones. Chop into serving pieces and discard the bones and bay leaves.

Bring the broth back to a boil.

If using lasagna noodles, cut them into thick strips or use as they are, as desired. Prepare the noodles according to package directions, but cook them in the broth. Be careful not to overcook.

Using a slotted spoon, remove the noodles and place on a warm serving platter.

Place the meat over the noodles. Top with onions.

Pour a little of the broth over the meat.

Garnish with chives or dill, and serve. Serves 4.

BORSOK (KYRGYZSTANI FRIED DOUGH)

These little breads can be served with honey or jam, or alongside dinner.

2 cups (240 grams) flour
½ tablespoon salt
¼ teaspoon sugar
¼ teaspoon yeast
¾ cup (180 milliliters) warm milk
   (warm the milk to about 110˚F, or
   43˚C)
1 egg
½ cup (120 mL) cooking oil

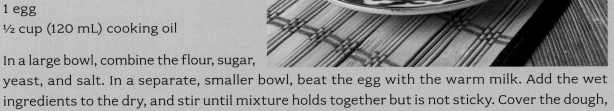

In a large bowl, combine the flour, sugar, yeast, and salt. In a separate, smaller bowl, beat the egg with the warm milk. Add the wet ingredients to the dry, and stir until mixture holds together but is not sticky. Cover the dough, and place it in a warm place in the kitchen for about 2 hours.

Roll the dough out on a floured surface to about a ¼-inch (6.35 millimeters) thickness. Cut the dough into 2-inch (5 centimeter) squares.

Pour about ¼ cup of the oil into a frying pan, and heat on medium high. Additional oil may be needed depending on the size of the pan.

Fry the borsok in the pan, adjusting the heat carefully so they cook without browning too quickly. Fry each piece, without overlapping, until it puffs up and is golden brown on the bottom. Flip each piece over to fry the other side until it is also golden brown.

Add additional oil as needed to keep a thin coat of oil on the surface of the pan.

Remove to a platter lined with paper towels and let cool.

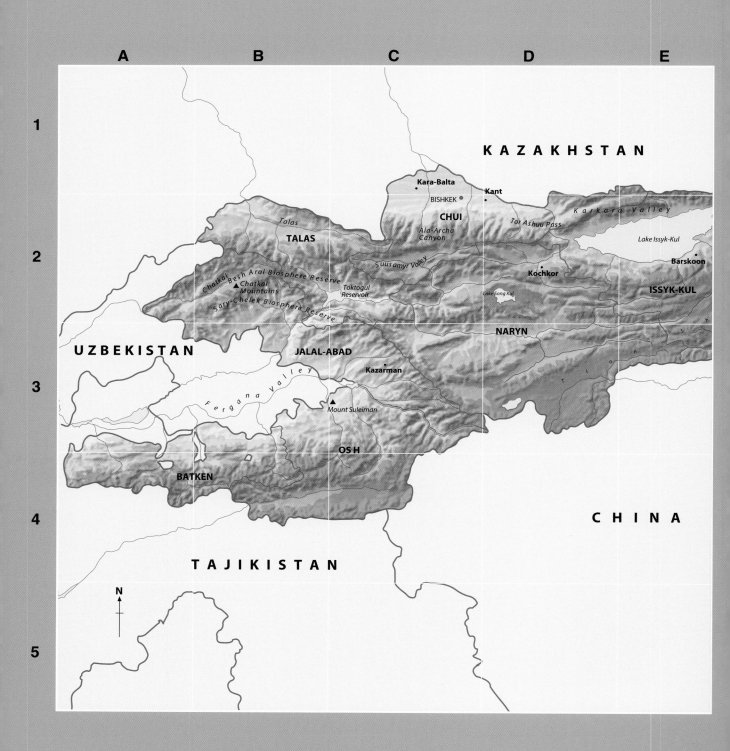

F

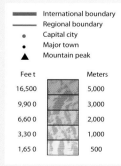

International boundary
Regional boundary
• Capital city
• Major town
▲ Mountain peak

Feet		Meters
16,500		5,000
9,900		3,000
6,600		2,000
3,300		1,000
1,650		500

ECONOMIC KYRGYZSTAN

Natural Resources

 Coal

 Fish

 Gold

 Hydroelectric Power

 Walnuts

Manufacturing

 Food Products

 Machinery and Instruments

Services

 Airport

 Tourism

Agriculture

 Cotton

 Grain

 Horticulture

 Livestock

Racehorses

Tobacco

Vineyards

ABOUT THE ECONOMY

All figures are 2017 estimates unless otherwise noted.

GROSS DOMESTIC PRODUCT (GDP, OFFICIAL EXCHANGE RATE)
$7.5 billion

GDP GROWTH RATE
4.6 percent

GDP BY SECTOR
agriculture: 14.6 percent
industry: 31.2 percent
services: 54.2 percent

INFLATION RATE
3.2 percent

PER CAPITA INCOME
$3,700

LABOR FORCE
2.841 million

UNEMPLOYMENT RATE
7.1 percent

POPULATION BELOW POVERTY LINE
32.1 percent (2015)

CURRENCY
$1 = 79.54 Kyrgyzstani som (KRG) (April 2020)
banknotes: 20, 50, 100, 200, 500, 1000, 5000 som
coins: 1, 3, 5, 10 som

NATURAL RESOURCES
abundant hydropower; gold; rare earth elements; locally exploitable coal, oil, and natural gas; other deposits of nepheline, mercury, bismuth, lead, and zinc

AGRICULTURAL PRODUCTS
cotton, potatoes, vegetables, grapes, fruits and berries; sheep, goats, cattle, wool

INDUSTRIES
small machinery, textiles, food processing, cement, shoes, lumber, refrigerators, furniture, electric motors

IMPORTS
oil and gas, machinery and equipment, chemicals, foodstuffs

IMPORT PARTNERS
China 32.6 percent, Russia 24.8 percent, Kazakhstan 16.4 percent, Turkey 4.8 percent, United States 4.2 percent

EXPORTS
gold, cotton, wool, garments, meat, mercury, uranium, electricity, machinery, shoes

EXPORT PARTNERS
Switzerland 59.1 percent, Uzbekistan 9.4 percent, Kazakhstan 5.1 percent, Russia 4.9 percent, UK 4 percent

CULTURAL KYRGYZSTAN

Manas Celebration Complex
Built in Talas—where the legend is said to have occurred—for the 1,000th anniversary of the Manas Epic, it is now used for official state functions.

Ala-Archa Canyon
This is a spectacular waterfall and glacier.

Museum of Fine Arts
This museum in Bishkek houses a wide variety of Kyrgyz folk art and large wall hangings.

National Historical Museum
This displays artifacts from the Bronze Age to the 20th century.

Chabana Festival
This annual gathering of herders and Kyrgyz cowboys includes horseback games and a large bazaar.

Lake Issyk-Kul
The northern shore is developing a major tourist economy.

Petroglyphs
Central Asia's greatest display of petroglyphs, some dating back 4,000 years, is found near Kazarman.

Russian Orthodox Cathedral
This replaced the country's first Christian church, which was in a yurt.

Mount Suleiman
Above the city of Osh, this large, jagged rock is a place of pilgrimage for Muslims, who believe the prophet Muhammad once prayed there.

Silk Road Museum
It has weapons and other relics dating back 2,000 years.

Lake Song Kul
Tourist yurt camps are located in the Song Kul zoological reserve, where rare animals and birds are protected.

Sarala-Saz
This is a high mountain pasture (jailoo) where visitors take horseback treks through beautiful country. Horseback games are played each August.

Ak Orgo Yurt Workshop
It takes 27 workers two months to build one yurt. (Price: $4,000)

Livestock Bazaar
The bazaar at Karakol is lively, noisy, crowded, and exciting.

ABOUT THE CULTURE

All figures are 2020 estimates unless otherwise noted.

OFFICIAL NAME
Kyrgyz Republic

CAPITAL
Bishkek

OTHER MAJOR CITIES
Jalal-Abad, Karakol, Naryn, Osh

FLAG
a red background with a yellow sun in the center, upon which is a yellow tunduk (the framework surrounding the smoke hole at the apex of a yurt) symbolizing hospitality, national identity, and nomadic life

POPULATION
5,965,000

POPULATION GROWTH RATE
0.96 percent

URBANIZATION
urban population: 36.9 percent of total population

ETHNIC GROUPS
Kyrgyz 73.5 percent, Uzbek 14.7 percent, Russian 5.5 percent, Dungan 1.1 percent, other 5.2 percent (includes Uyghur, Tajik, Turk, Kazakh, Tatar, Ukrainian, Korean, German) (2019)

RELIGIONS
Muslim 90 percent (majority Sunni), Christian 7 percent (Russian Orthodox 3 percent), other 3 percent (includes Jewish, Buddhist, Baha'i)

LANGUAGES
Kyrgyz (official) 71.4 percent, Uzbek 14.4 percent, Russian (official) 9 percent, other 5.2 percent (2009)

INFANT MORTALITY RATE
23.3 deaths per 1,000 live births

LIFE EXPECTANCY
men: 67.7 years
women: 76.2 years

LITERACY RATE
99.6 percent

TIMELINE

IN KYRGYZSTAN	IN THE WORLD

100 BCE
The Silk Road is formed.

117 CE
The Roman Empire reaches its greatest extent.

700 CE
Arab invaders conquer Central Asia and introduce Islam.

900–1200s
Kyrgyz people migrate southward from central Siberia to the Tian Shan region.

1530
The transatlantic slave trade begins.

1620
The Pilgrims sail the *Mayflower* to America.

1685–1758
Mongol Oyrats rule present-day Kyrgyzstan.

1758–1862
Various khans rule parts of Kyrgyzstan. Russians seize Pishpek Fort (modern Bishkek); Russia rules most of Kyrgyzstan.

1776
U.S. Declaration of Independence is written.

1789–1799
The French Revolution takes place.

1861
The American Civil War begins.

1914–1918
World War I takes place.

1917–1923
The Russian Revolution topples monarchy and creates the Soviet Union.

1924
Kyrgyzstan is brought into the Soviet Union.

1928–1932
The Kyrgyz are forced to give up nomadic ways and move onto collective farms.

1930s
Kyrgyz intelligentsia who express dissent are imprisoned or executed.

1936
The Kyrgyz Soviet Socialist Republic (Kirghiziya) becomes a republic within the Soviet Union.

1939–1945
Soviet factories are moved from the western Soviet Union to Kyrgyzstan.

1939–1945
World War II takes place.

1966–1969
The Chinese Cultural Revolution takes place.

IN KYRGYZSTAN	IN THE WORLD
1991	**1991**
Kyrgyzstan declares independence; Askar Akayev becomes president.	The Soviet Union breaks up.
	2001
2005	Terrorist attacks on the United States take place on September 11.
In the Tulip Revolution, Akayev is forced from office.	
2008	**2008**
A major earthquake in Osh kills at least 65 people.	The United States elects its first African American president, Barack Obama.
2009	**2009**
Journalist Gennady Pavluk is murdered.	An outbreak of H1N1 flu spreads around the world.
2010	
Protests sweep President Kurmanbek Bakiyev from power; ethnic clashes happen in Osh and Jalal-Abad; a new constitution is written; and Kyrgyzstan becomes a parliamentary republic.	
2011	
Prime Minister Almazbek Atambayev wins the presidential election.	
2013	
Protestors blockade the Kumtor gold mine.	
2014	
The United States closes its air base at Manas.	
	2015–2016
	ISIS launches terror attacks in Belgium and France.
2017	**2017**
Sooronbay Jeenbekov is elected president.	Donald Trump becomes the U.S. president. Hurricanes devastate Caribbean islands.
2019	**2019**
Former president Atambayev is arrested in a dramatic raid on his compound and charged with murder and plotting a government coup.	Notre Dame Cathedral in Paris is damaged by fire. President Trump is impeached.
2020	**2020**
An incident on the Kyrgyz-Tajik border wounds three Kyrgyz soldiers. Major cities are shut down to fight the COVID-19 pandemic.	The COVID-19 pandemic spreads across the world.

GLOSSARY

akim
The head man, or chief, of a tribe.

ak-kalpak
A white felt cap with embroidery and a tassel; the standard headgear for Kyrgyz men.

akyn
A traditional songwriter and performer.

chaykana
A Kyrgyz teahouse.

equestrian
Relating to horseback riding.

fundamentalism
The belief in an extreme form of a religion.

jailoo
A high summer pasture.

kok boru
A game played on horseback, with a headless goat carcass as the object to be carried into a circle.

komuz
A three-stringed instrument played by plucking.

kymyz
A beverage made from fermented mare's milk.

mal bazari
The popular Sunday bazaar for buying and selling livestock in Kyrgyzstan.

manaschi
An akyn who has special skills in narrating the Manas Epic.

Nowruz
One of Kyrgyzstan's most popular festivals; also known as "New Day."

oblast
An administrative province of Kyrgyzstan.

rayon
A regional district within an oblast.

secular
Not relating to or concerned with religion.

shaman
A practitioner who acts as an intermediary between the natural and supernatural worlds, using magic to cure illness, foretell the future, or control spiritual forces.

shyrdak
A handmade felt carpet that is Kyrgyzstan's best-known craft.

tunduk
The circular frame of wooden spokes that forms the apex of a yurt; also, the central symbol on the Kyrgyz flag.

yurt
The portable tentlike dwelling of nomadic Central Asians, still used in modern Kyrgyzstan.

FOR FURTHER INFORMATION

BOOKS

Fatland, Erika. *Sovietistan: A Journey Through Turkmenistan, Kazakhstan, Tajikistan, Kyrgyzstan and Uzbekistan*. London, UK: MacLehose Press, 2019.

Gillmore, Ged. *Stans By Me: A Whirlwind Tour Through Central Asia—Kazakhstan, Kyrgyzstan, Tajikistan, Turkmenistan and Uzbekistan*. New South Wales, Australia: deGrevilo Publishing, 2019.

Mitchell, Laurence. *Kyrgyzstan*. Chesham, UK: Bradt Travel Guides, 2019.

ONLINE

Al Jazeera. "Kyrgyzstan News." https://www.aljazeera.com/topics/country/kyrgyzstan.html.

BBC News. "Kyrgyzstan." https://www.bbc.com/news/topics/cvenzmgylw1t/kyrgyzstan.

CIA. *The World Factbook*. "Kyrgyzstan." https://www.cia.gov/library/publications/the-world-factbook/geos/kg.html.

Encyclopædia Britannica. "Kyrgyzstan." https://www.britannica.com/place/Kyrgyzstan.

Kabar News. http://en.kabar.kg.

MUSIC

Greenberg, Nurmira Salimbaeva. *My Kyrgyzstan*. CD Baby, 2014.

Kambarkan Folk Ensemble. *The Music of Kyrgyzstan*. ARC Music, 2003.

Tengir-Too. *Music of Central Asia Vol. 1: Tengir-Too Mountain Music of Kyrgyzstan*. Smithsonian Folkways Recordings, 2006.

VIDEO

The Light Thief. Global Lens, 2010.

Mythical Roads. "Season 1, Episode 1: The Road of the Nomadic Soul: From Kyrgyzstan to Tajikistan." Bo Travail, 2020.

The Silk Road, "Episode 10: Kyrgyzstan." Arte, 2016.

The Wildlife Conservation Project: Marco Polo Sheep. Firesteel Films, Inc., 2019.

BIBLIOGRAPHY

BBC News. "Kyrgyzstan Country Profile." https://www.bbc.com/news/world-asia-16186907.

BBC News. "Kyrgyzstan Profile—Timeline." https://www.bbc.com/news/world-asia-16185772.

CIA. *The World Factbook*. "Kyrgyzstan." https://www.cia.gov/library/publications/the-world -factbook/geos/kg.html.

Encyclopædia Britannica. "Kyrgyzstan." https://www.britannica.com/place/Kyrgyzstan.

Food and Agriculture Organization of the United Nations. "The Kyrgyz Republic: Country Fact Sheet on Food and Agriculture Policy Trends." February 2018. http://www.fao.org/3/I8701EN/ i8701en.pdf.

Freedom House. "Kyrgyzstan." https://freedomhouse.org/country/kyrgyzstan.

Giles, Malika. "UNESCO Recognizes Kyrgyz Epic of Manas." *Moscow Times,* December 8, 2013. https://www.themoscowtimes.com/2013/12/08/unesco-recognizes-kyrgyz- epic-of-manas-a30280.

Library of Congress, Federal Research Division. "Country Profile: Kyrgyzstan." January 2007. https://www.loc.gov/rr/frd/cs/profiles/Kyrgyzstan-new.pdf.

Pierobon, Chiara. "Policy Brief: Preventing Violent Extremism in Kyrgyzstan: the Role of the International Donor Community." OSCE Academy in Bishtek, March 2020. http://osce-academy. net/upload/file/Chiara_Pierobon.pdf.

Pomfret, Richard. "Exploiting a Natural Resource in a Poor Country: The Good, the Bad and the Ugly Sides of the Kyrgyz Republic's Gold Mine." IOS, May 2018, https://www.econstor.eu/ bitstream/10419/178999/1/102061918X.pdf.

Sharkov, Damien. "This Country Is Changing Its Stalin-Imposed Alphabet After 80 Years." *Newsweek,* February 20, 2018. https://www.newsweek.com/kazakhstan-changing-russian- alphabet-812178.

Snow Leopard Trust. snowleopard.org.

Stratfor Worldview. "Central Asia: The Complexities of the Fergana Valley." October 7, 2013. https://worldview.stratfor.com/article/central-asia-complexities-fergana-valley.

UNESCO Intangible Cultural Heritage of Humanity. "Kyrgyzstan." https://ich.unesco.org/en/ state/kyrgyzstan-KG.

UNESCO World Heritage. "Kyrgyzstan." https://whc.unesco.org/en/statesparties/kg.

World Economic Forum. "Global Gender Gap Report 2020." http://reports.weforum.org/global- gender-gap-report-2020/dataexplorer/#economy=KGZ.

INDEX

INDEX